HOTEL FRONT OFFICE EXECUTIVE IN A MINUTE

A PRACTICAL APPROCH

DR GAJANAN SHIRKE

This book is dedicated to all hospitality front desk employees

Contents

Preface

Hotel Front office Executive in a Minute is ready reference manual aims to train and empower students and professionals with essentials of front office services in the hospitality industry. The book aims to explore all the relevant aspects and issues related to front office operations and management with the help of numerous industry-related examples, cases and project assignments.

Acknowledgements

I would like to express a special debt of gratitude to my wife Rajeshree and my two daughters Rupeshi & Kavya

About Author

Gajanan Shirke, a hotel consultant, has years of extensive experience in the hospitality industry. His thirst for learning and aspiration to become a multi-faceted expert in the hotel industry helped him rise from employment to becoming an independent professional in the hospitality sector. Since his last assignment as General Manager at Kamat Hotels, he has become a renowned hotel consultant with a proven track record of developing, training and growing some of the best-known hotels, restaurants and fast-food joints in the Indian market. He was appointed as an expert consultant for The Eighth meeting of the Board of Studies for Hotel Management & Catering Technology. He is a visiting faculty at various Hotel Management Colleges and has trained over a thousand hospitality professionals. He has completed numerous pre and post opening hotel consultancies in India and overseas.

In order to spread his extensive knowledge to aspiring hotel professionals, Gajanan has penned a large number of books spanning different segments of the hospitality industry. Starting from his first book 'Bar Management and Operations' published in 2010, he has written 50 books including Hospitality Management, Food and Beverage Management, Hotel Engineering Management, Front Office Management, Hotel Housekeeping Management, The Cookery Trilogy: Advance Cookery Theory, The Cookery Trilogy: Foundation of Cookery, The Cookery Trilogy: The Basic Cookery Book, Hotel Sales and Marketing, Hospitality Industry Accounting & Fundamentals, Customer Interaction Excellence in Hospitality, History of Indian Cuisine – Volume 1, History of Indian Cuisine – Volume 2, Hotel Owner's Manual, Hotel Security & Prevention, Training Manager's Manual, Exceptional Service In Hospitality Six Sigma Way, etc.

Contents

CHAPTER ONE

Front Office department

Front Office department Layout

A well designed and laid Front office can have a great effect on the efficiency of the department and the well being of the staff. The basic aims when planning the Front office should be,

- Maximum customer contact without endangering the security of cash, keys, records and information.
- The minimization of effort in processing a guest stays from the original reservation to the point of departure.
- The flow of work involved should be reflected in the positioning of equipment, and the various functions.

The front office consists of two main areas.

1. Guest contact Area
2. Back of House Area

Guest Contact Area: This area consists of Reception, Registration, Cash, information, bell desk, Guest Relations desk, lobby managers desk, and travel counter (optional). They are located in the areas accessible to guests.

Back of house Area: This area consists of Telephone operation room, Front office manager's office, Reservations office, Baggage room and safe deposit boxes.(Optional). These departments are in the back area and are not immediately in guest access area. They are considered vital support services sections of the front office.

Guest Contact Areas

Hotel Entrance: The main entrance of a hotel must be easily identifiable and lead to the front desk. An entrance should be clearly defined and should provide a good view of the enterer. The doors should be quite large to facilitate to enter and leave the hotel building easily.

Hotel Lobby: This includes a waiting area leading to the reception. The Cashiers desk, information Counter, Guest Relations desk and Lobby Managers desk, which combines to do service to the front office of the hotel, are located here. The lobby also serves as an assembling point for guests. The Reception desk should be very noticeable to the lobby. The lobby should be attractive as it is the area from which a person forms the first impression of the hotel. The entire constructions and decoration should be done, bearing in mind the extent and nature of traffic, appearance, cleaning, maintenance, safety, noise, comfort and cost.

Reception Counter/desk: This section handles the selling of rooms to guests. It also handles allocations of rooms, and amendments to guest stays. It maintains statistics and provides information to other departments of the hotel as well.

Split-level Reception Desk: The reception counter is located in the lobby. Most counters would be in two different levels. The side, which the guest uses higher level counter and the lower counter is used by the receptionist. This is to ensure safety and convenience for the receptionists. In medium and large hotels the reception section, porterage and information section, billing and the cash desk can also be a part of the counter and at the same level, instead of separate counters. In some hotels, especially if they are large, there may be a separate counter for cash and billing sections.

Guest Relations Desk: This is an elegant small office table with many drawers normally situated at a corner of lobby on the opposite side of the main (Reception) counter used to help guests with any and all issues they may have. It is situated in such a way to observe guest movements easily as well as other service providers in the guest contact zone. They coordinate all day to day matters at the Front office, in addition to maintain guest relation activities.

Porterage and Information (Concierge): This section handles guest luggage (incoming out going and left behind). It undertakes various services such as providing information supplying news papers, selling picture postcards & stamps, receiving and handling mail, paging guests, etc. staff working in this area should be knowledgeable and should have information such as railway time tables, flight schedules and Road Maps, and all information pertaining to hotel and destination that guests may regularly request.

Cash Desk: All current guest bills are kept up to-date in this section. The guest vouchers (credit bills) are posted into the appropriate guest accounts. This counter is usually partitioned with glass for security reasons. The cashier encashes foreign currency, receives payment from the guests, issue receipts for payments, maintains safe custody of guest valuables, handles guest disbursements (paid outs).

Travel Desk: Usually this is a sourced out facility manned by staff that are from the travel company. They would arrange taxis, buses and van for hire with or without chauffeurs. Also would offer tour itineraries.

Backup Service Area

Reservations Office: This is usually located in a room behind the reception counter/desk area, away from the guest view. The positioning is to facilitate smooth & easy operation in liaising with the reception staff. This department handles all reservations and correspondence concerning them. In addition to many telephone lines, there can be, Fax machine and email facilities, and computer stations for central reservation system and internet access, if necessary, in this office for communication regarding reservations.

Telephone Operators Room: It is located in a room close to the lobby, and away from the view of the guest. It should be in a quite environment so that, the telephone operators are not disturbed by outsiders. The telephone exchange is usually air-conditioned and has a low temperature due to the sensitive nature of the switching equipment.

Front Office Manager's Room: It is an office that the front office manager occupies, to carryout his duties. His office should be within close proximity to all front office areas as he is overall in charge of the front office department.

Front Office Equipment

Front Office Equipment can be divided into two types.

a. Manual Equipment
b. Electronic equipment

Manual Equipment: Besides modern equipment such as computers, the following conventional equipments are used in a large number of hotels in

Sri Lanka as well as in other countries due to their low cost and ease in operation.

- Key and Mail rack
- Reception Board/ Room rack
- Reservations rack

Key and Mail Rack: It was until recently a standard piece of equipment in almost all the hotels. It is still used in many Sri Lankan hotels. The key and mail rack has pigeonholes corresponding to the number of rooms in the hotel. Each room number has a corresponding pigeonhole, with its number on it. The guest keys (when not with guests or in use otherwise) are kept there as well as guest mail and correspondence. The shape and size of the key and mail rack varies from one hotel to another, depending on the size of the hotel, the size of the reception counter area and interior décor of the particular hotel. The key and mail rack is in numerical sequence, a systematical arrangement of rooms and floors to enable receptionists to locate the desired pigeonhole without delay.

Operation: The original keys of rooms are kept in the key and mail rack. They are given to guests from it, on arrival and are collected when guests depart. During their stay, guests are requested to leave their room keys at the reception counter whenever they go out of the hotel, and collect same upon their return, during which time the receptionists keep the guest's keys at the key and mail rack.

When mail and messages are received for guests, the receptionists "time-stamps" them, locates the guests on the alphabetical index, and writes the room number on the envelope. The mail is then placed in the pigeonhole corresponding to the guest's room. Packages that are too large for the pigeonhole are stored elsewhere, and a message is placed in the appropriate pigeonhole, indicating that a parcel awaits collection.

In older hotels, the key and mail rack is visible to any one who comes towards the reception counter, as it was fixed on the wall that was just behind. But now in newer hotels, it is fixed in the counter itself, away from the view of outsiders, mainly for security reasons as others may get to notice the whereabouts of guests (i.e. If the key is in the rack, the guest is not in the room etc).

Reception Board/room Rack/room Status Rack: The reception board/ Room rack/ Room status rack provides a visual indication of room status at any given time. The receptionists can at a glance ascertain whether the room is vacant or not, and the name and particulars of a guest occupying the room. The room rack should have a number of pockets/slots arranged according the floors, and equal to the number of rooms in the hotel/ these are arranged in vertical or horizontal order. Due to space limitations in most hotels it is mostly vertically arranged. Each slot/pocket has a corresponding room number.

1) When a room is occupied a rack slip is filled out with the following particulars; Name of guest, the terms, duration of stay and number of people occupying the room. This slip is then inserted to slot corresponding to the room number given to the guest.

OCCUPIED

Room No .... Until.........................

Name of Guest :...

Meal Plan ....No of Pax:...................

Date...................... Signature..........................

Enter Caption

2) On the day of departure, the room slip is may be folded in half placed on the slot. No sooner the departure takes place the slip will be removed.

3) On room change the slip is altered accordingly and is moved from the slot of the previous room to the present room.

4) If a room is out of order a special slip is usually printed in red and placed in the slot until such time the room is readied.

OUT OF ORDER

Room No .... Until...............................
Reason

____

____

____

____

Date............................... Signature...............................

Enter Caption

5) If a room is house used or held off, more or less the same procedure is adapted, (as for out of order rooms) a special card could be used the purpose.

BLOCKED

Room No .... Until...............................
Reason

____

____

____

____

Date............................... Signature...............................

Enter Caption

6) Receptionists on the night shift or early morning shift would go through the rack and fold rack slips of guests due to check out next day/ day beginning. The receptionist in duty in the morning, then going through the folded slip will know which guests are going to check out and will be able to handle it better (get ready with the departure Procedure). This situation also makes it easier it prepare departures list, particularly if you have a large number of guests.

7). Allocating of rooms, too, can be done on the reception board. Special room allocation (rack) slips are inserted and partially lifted in the slot. In times of high occupancy this is particularly important because allocation can be then done not only in vacant ready rooms but also on already occupied due out room by inserting a rack slip lifted, but behind the existing one.

RESERVED

Room No .... Until...

Name of Guest :...

Meal Plan ....No of Pax:................................

Date.. Signature...

Enter Caption

8) Different colored cards could be used to identify different groups etc. who are staying in the hotel. Also separate colors can be used for F.I.T. s V.I.P. s and so on.

9) It is Important to up date the reception board each time a change in room status takes place. Otherwise it would give wrong information.

The Location

The reception board is fixed and recessed in the reception counter, facing the receptionist (& not the guest) at a 60 degree angle (approx.). So that it is not visible to guests, but at all times in direct view of the receptionists.

Electronic Equipments

Electronic equipments take the shape of computerized equipments that help the workflow of the Front Office Department. The systems that are available are mostly computer based. Most hotels would have a main computer with a lot of work stations for each area of the hotel.

1. POS or Point of Sales systems – These are systems that are computer based and today mostly are equipped with touch screen facilities. There are menu options displayed on the computer screen and one only has to touch the selection and the computer can pick it up. They are mostly used for billing, room, restaurant and other areas. It will then send the info to accounts, stores, kitchen etc. so that all information is shared instantly at the time of guest order.

1. PMS or Property Management Systems - These systems are made up of several different modules of system software put together. Each module looks after one particular aspect of the management of a hotel property. The number and scale of each module would depend much on the size and level of service of the individual hotel or property. Typical examples of modules are;

   1. property management,
   2. sales and catering,
   3. quality management,
   4. accounting
   5. room management
   6. Function space sales, etc.

3. CRM or Customer Relationship Management Systems - The Customer Relationship Management systems are designed to track all relationships with guests to improve guest service and marketing. All guest visits are tracked with information on guest details, personal preferences, likes dislikes etc. So each time a guest comes to the hotel, the staff has a way of finding out the basic information and the likes and dislikes of each guest.

This can be used to build a close relationship with guests as well as to anticipate the guest needs and wants in advance.

<u>EQUIPMENTS USED IN FRONT OFFICE OPERATIONS</u>

Any department of a hotel requires some kind of equipments to run that particular department efficiently.

A large number of factors play a very important role in the choice of equipments to keep in the Front Office of a hotel to carry out day-to-day administration and management of the department.

The equipments used in Front Office are mainly classified into 3 segments:

1. FULLY AUTOMATED EQUIPMENTS:

(i) CREDIT CARD VALIDATOR: The credit card validator is automated front office equipment used by the Front office cashier to check the validity of the credit card presented by the guest as a mode of payment at the time of departure. This equipment is linked to a credit card data bank, which holds information concerning the validity of the C.C. of the guest. This equipment helps the hotel to know the validity as well as the balance of the credit card, which is, offends by the guest thus reducing the chances of loss to the hotel.

(ii) TIME-STAMPING MACHINE: This is an electronic device, which is used extensively by the Front Office of a hotel. The machine imprints the details of a guest on a piece of paper like check in and out time, any message etc. This equipment is very helpful to the hotel as it ease out the operations of the Front office department to maintain the records and other data pertaining to the guests.

(iii) FAX MACHINES: The full form of the Fax is Facsimile Automated Xerox machine and is an important electronic equipment used in the Front desk for the purpose of communication. This equipment operates through telephonic lines and is used extensively to receive or send official documents, which are important from the point of view of guest and also the hotel.

(iv) CALL ACCOUNTING SYSTEM: The call accounting system is called APBX (Automated Private Branch Exchange) is used in Telephone exchange section of the front office department to automatically trace and bill the outgoing calls made by the guests during their stay in the hotel.

(v) COMPUTER: Almost all the hotels of the world is using computer these dates for the successful operations of the hotel. A computer is very essential equipment where one can feed various data and information pertaining to the guests. Computer these days are installed with the special software like Fidalio, POS, IDS etc. which has all the inputs data and formats of the hotel operations and thus easing out the work of audit and control of the hotel.

2. SEMI-AUTOMATED EQUIPMENTS:

(i) POSTING MACHINE: Posting machine is very essential equipment used in the Front Office for posting the various charges in the accounts of the guests. The posting machine is generally used to calculate the totals of the guests' accounts, departments and transactions.

(ii) CASH REGISTER: The cash register is semi-automated equipment used generally by the Front desk such as stamps, newspapers, candy etc.

(iii) WAKE UP CALLS: The most famous and common wake up device is known as the "James Remindo Timer". In this all the wake up request from the guests are feeded into this times monitoring the date, time, room no., name of guest and the telephone of that particular room automatically rings at the mentioned time thus waking up the guest.

(iv) CREDIT CARD IMPRINTER: This device is mostly used by the Front Office cashier at the time of arrival, when the guest presents this credit card to the cashier as the mode of payment of his hotel bills. All the details of the credit card is imprinted on the paper with the help of the device.

3. MANUAL EQUIPMENTS:

(i) ROOM RACK: Room rack is a large wooden framework located just behind the front desk. It contains a metallic array of pockets, which contains large number of room rack slips for showing the reservation and house keeping status of each guest room of a hotel. It is a joint effort of the front desk and housekeeping to timely update the room rack in order to have an accurate room status position.

(ii) INFORMATION RACK: This is again an important device present at the front desk, which contains all the required information of in-house guests in an alphabetical order. The information rack is a revolving device, which enables front office assistant to know the details of guests, which are staying in the hotel, like name, room no., arrival date, date of departure etc.

(iii) MAIL & MESSAGE RACK: Mail or message rack is a wooden framework present at the front desk, which has pigeonholes mentioning each room number of the hotel. Any message for in-house guest is noted on the message slip and then put in the pigeonhole of the room no. in which that particular guest is staying.

(iv) KEY RACK OR KEY DRAWER: Key rack or key drawer is a wooden or metallic framework present underneath the front desk. It contains an array of slots used for keeping the keys of the guest rooms in sequential order for the guest rooms present in the hotel. Nowadays most good hotels are using the electronic keys for their guest rooms, but for hotels, which are still persisting with the metallic keys, the key rack is an important device to maintain the control of keys.

(v) FOLIOWELL OR FOLIO BUCKET: This is important equipment used in the front desk cash section. This equipment contains a large number of slots where the folios are arranged. Sequentially according to the room number. The folio well is used by the front office cashier to store and track the folios of the various registered guests of the hotel and is used to maintain the folios safely for future use and reference.

CHAPTER TWO

Front Office Organization

Importance of Front Office

(Why front office is called the Nerve Center of the hotel)

Front office can be defined as a front of the house department located around the lobby area of a hospitality industry.

Since this department is situated in the lobby of the hotel and is visible to the guests and visitors at the front of the hotel, it is called " front office department".

Front office is one of the major operational and revenue producing department of the hotel which generates two third of the revenue earned by the hotel from the sale of guest rooms.

The front office in a hotel is the department responsible for the sale of hotel rooms through systematic methods of reservation, followed by registration and assigning rooms to the guests. The term "sale of room" may appear misleading to those unfamiliar with the industry, sale here means the use of hotel room at a price for the mentioned no. of days.

Room tariff i.e. rate charged per room is computed for a particular day and ends at 12:00 hrs. The front Office in a Hotel holds prime importance in view of the basic nature of the hotel i.e. to sell rooms. As rooms are the most perishable commodity of the hotel, hence the importance of front Office is more as compared to the other departments of hotel.

Front office may be called as nerve center of the hotel, since it is the department, which is easily approachable by the guest as it is in the front area. Hence all other departments are linked directly to front office regarding the needs and complaints of the guest. It is just like a heart of the hotel through which all other departments are linked as nerves.

Since it is well known phrase that "first impression is that last impression", and the first impression of the hotel on the guest is through front office department. Therefore Front office is the most important section of the Hotel

FRONT OFFICE ORGANIZATION Departmental Hierarchy

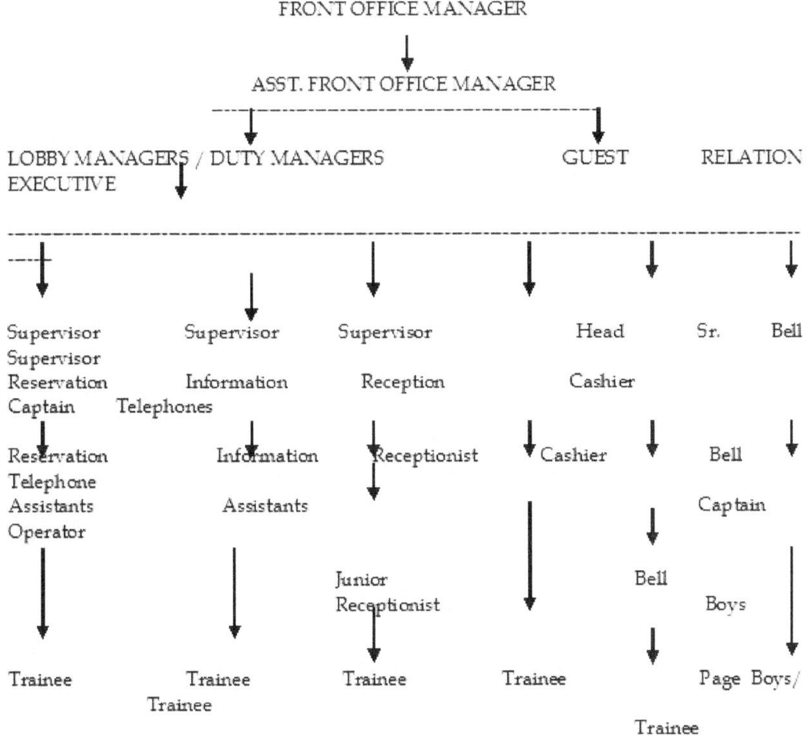

Enter Caption

FUNCTIONAL ORGANIZATION OF FRONT OFFICE DEPARTMENT

Front Office Organization is divided into divisions. The divisions of Front Office are:

(a) RESERVATION: This section is responsible for reserving the rooms for the prospective guest. This section is also responsible for cancellation and amendment of room bookings.

(b) RECEPTION / REGISTRATION: This section is responsible for welcoming guests on arrival; the section is also responsible for registering the guests on arrival. Registering of guest is a statutory obligation for any organization engaged in accommodation business.

(c) INFORMATION: Front office has a very important segment called Information desk. This section is the nerve center of the hotel and should be easily approachable by all the hotel guests for their queries and information.

(d) CASH & BILLS: This section is responsible for maintaining the statement of expenditure (guest bill or guest folio) for a resident guest. This section is also responsible for settlement of guest bills on departure.

(e) BELL DESK: This section is responsible for handling guest baggage at the time of arrival, at the time of departure.

(f) TELEPHONES: This is responsible for all incoming and outgoing calls both for the guests and management.

<u>Normally Front Office is divided into two categories</u>

- Front Office, which consist of Reception, Information Desk, Bell Desk and Cashiers.
- Back office, which consist of Reservation & telephones.

TYPE OF ROOMS

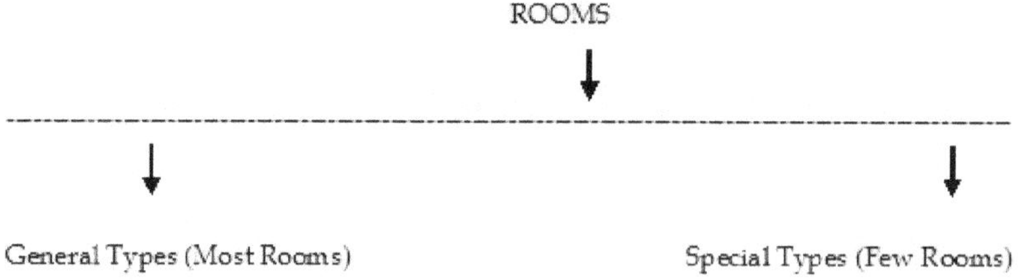

Enter Caption

A. GENERAL TYPE ROOMS

(a) Single Room: oom with a single bed and meant for the accommodation of one person Abbreviation: "SGL" Symbol: "-"bed of the size of approximately 36"x 76".

(b) Twin Room: It is a room meant for two persons having two single beds separated from each other. Abbreviation: "TBR" Symbol: "="

(c) Double Room: It is a room meant for two persons having one double bed. Abbreviation: "DBL" Symbol: "+"bed of the size of approximately 54"x76, or two single joined together.

(d) Suite: It is an apartment having a bedroom with a double bed and a living room. Besides the room numbers every suite has got a name depending upon the décor, theme etc, like ITC Maurya Sheraton has suits by the name of Mauryan dynasty like: Ashoka, Emperor, Chandragupta etc. The furniture and fittings are generally quite costly. Symbol: "S"

B. SPECIAL TYPE ROOMS

(a) Junior Suite: When a big room is converted into a suite with the help of a partition; it is known as a Junior Suite.

(b) Pent House: It is a suite, which is situated at the terrace level, and a part of it is open to the sky.

(c) Cabana Room: It is a room situated away from the main building, is near to the swimming pool. Room is mainly used for changing purposes. A cabana may not have a bed. A temporary bar is optional. A cabana is rented as hourly basis.

(d) Duplex: It is a room having two levels. The upper level is used as a bedroom and the lower level is used as a parlour or living room. The two levels are connected through a staircase.

(e) Hospitality Room: It is a room where a resident guest can entertain their own guest. The hospitality room has no bed. They are rented on hourly basis and are mainly available with commercial hotels.

(f) Efficiency Room: It is a room with kitchen facilities. They are usually available in resort hotel because most of the guest requires these rooms as they are on a special diet.

(g) Hollywood Twin Bedded Room: It is a twin room with two single beds separated from each other, but having a common head board.

(h) Studio Room: It is a single room with one or more sofa, which can be converted into a bed.

(i) Murphy Bedded Room: It is a room having a Murphy bed. (It is a bed, which can be folded against the wall).

TARIFF PLANS

Food plan or meal plan is a composite package offered by Front office department, which includes accommodation and meals.

MAJOR TARIFF / FOOD PLANS ARE:

(i) EUROPEAN PLAN: Under this plan, guest is offered only accommodation. E.M.T. (Early Morning Tea) is optional depending upon the policy of the hotel.

(ii) CONTINENTAL PLAN (C.P.): Under this plan, the guest is offered a continental breakfast along with the accommodation. E.M.T. is again optional. Continental breakfast is the lightest breakfast, which includes: Fruit juices, break basket with preserves & Tea/Coffee.

(iii) BERMUDA PLAN (B.P.): Under this plan, the guest is offered an American breakfast with accommodation. E.M.T. is again optional. American breakfast includes: Fruit juice, Cereals, Bread Basket with preserves, Eggs to order & Tea/Coffee.

(iv) AMERICAN PLAN (A.P.): This plan is also known as "Full boarding plan". Under this plan, guest is offered with 02 minor meals (i.e. breakfast & evening snacks) & 02 major meals (Lunch & Dinner) along with accommodation. E.M.T. is again optional.

(v) MODIFIED AMERICAN PLAN: Under this plan, the guest is offered with one minor meal and one major meal along with accommodation. E.M.T. is optional.

TARIFF CARD / TARIFF ROOM RATES:

It is compulsory for all kinds of hotel to display the tariff structure. In small hotels it is done through Tariff Board where the room rates are displayed in Reception. In 5 star hotels tariff plans are used, it is a small sized card where tariff according to the food plan is presented. It is available with reception and also available in each guest room.

Following are the information obtained from a Tariff card:

1. Rack rates according to food plan.

2. Govt. taxes as applicable eg. Luxury tax, sales tax etc.

3. Basis of charging room rent.

4. Brief description of facilities available in the hotel.

TYPES OF ROOM RENT:

1. RACK RATE: It is the rate printed on a tariff card. It is the highest equipped rate generally offered to Free Individual Travelers (F.I.T.).

2. PACKAGE RATE: This is a special rate which covers all expenses right from airport pick up and drops, meals, room rent, sight seeing etc. These package rates are normally set for a fix period of time eg. Weekend package, summer package, charismas package etc.

3. OFF SEASON RATE: This rate is normally offered in Resorts, where special discounted rates are offered to the tourists during off seasons eg. Off-season for Simla would be the winter months and off-season for Goa will be summer months.

4. EMPLOYEE DISCOUNTED RATES: In chain hotels, employee may be given discount on rack rates for the hotels belonging to that chain. Employee discounted rates would depend on the availability of space and

are generally offered during slack season.

5. PUBLICITY & PROMOTIONAL RATES: For publicity purposes, influential persons like Company Directors, Top Executives, Celebrities etc may be given discounts for the sake of publicity. These kinds of persons are known as C.I.P. (Commercially Important Person) from whom the hotel can expect business.

6. CORPORATE RATES: It is also known as C.G.V.R. (Company Guaranteed Volume Rates). Companies, which give regular business to the hotel, are given special discounted rates, which are known as Corporate Rates.

7. GROUP RATES: Special discounted rates are offered to groups of guest. Discount percentage would depend upon number of group members.

8. CREW MEMBER DISCOUNTED RATES: For airline crewmembers, discounted rats are offered by hotel based on the contract between Airline Company and the hotel.

9. FHRAI MEMBERS DISCOUNTED RATES: Federation of Hotels and Restaurant Association of India members are offered a discount up to 30% by hotels.

10. EXTRA BED RATE: A fix charge generally one fourth of the room is allowed to permit the extra bed in the same room.

EXAMPLE OF TARIFF CARD:

	E.P.	C.P.	B.P.	M.A.P	A.P
Single Occupancy	3000	3150	3200	3400	3600
Double Occupancy	3500	3650	3700	4000	4200
Suite Occupancy	5000	5200	5400	5600	6000

Enter Caption

NOTE: All Rack rates are (highest) room rates but all room rates are not rack rates.

TRANSACTIONAL ANALYSIS

There are 03 egos status with a human being:

(i) Parent Ego

(ii) Adult Ego

(iii) Child Ego

This analysis helps us to deal with the people (guests) irrespective of age and sex they belong to.

(i) PARENT EGO: When a person is in parent Ego, he thinks he is intelligent and can influence other persons. This person is said to be in Parent ego, eg. giving suggestions, advice etc.

Enter Caption

Where 'X' is the ego of guest and 'Y' is the ego the second person.

(ii) ADULT EGO: When a person talks logically and the level of thinking is same as that of a person with whom he is communicates. He is said to be in Adult ego.

Enter Caption

(iii) CHILD EGO: When a person behaves emotionally. He is said to be in Child ego.

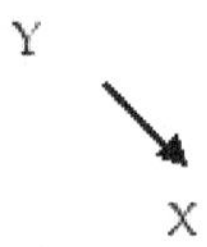

Enter Caption

Only one type of ego stays as active at a particular time. Age also plays an important role to determine which ego state is likely to be active.

In hotels we have to keep the adult ego active. Most of guest (99.9% approx.) has their adult ego active and hence we don't have any problems in dealing with them as they understand logic and talk sense.

Unfortunately 0.1% guest has their adult ego inactive.

If guest is in parent ego, we cannot shift our adult ego to parent ego but we have to bring down the guests' parent ego to adult ego, so that the communication becomes in straight line.

So guests are normally divided into 02 main segments:

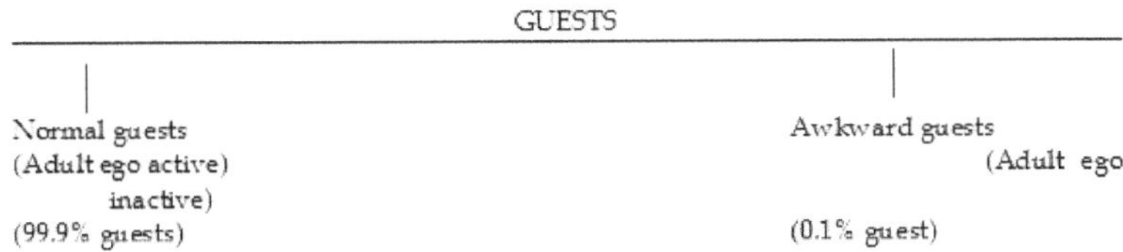

Enter Caption

AWKWARD GUESTS ARE DIVIDED INTO VARIOUS CATEGORIES:

(a) ANGRY GUESTS: There anger can be compared with the steam in a pressure cooker. If one tries to block the steam of cooker, it will burst, so do the angry guest.

Rules could be:

(i) Do not interrupt

(ii) Listen to them

(iii) Let the steam cool

(iv) Apologize

(v) Take prompt action in front of the guest.

(vi) Follow up

(b) SNOB GUESTS: These guests are in parent ego and are suffering from superiority complex. These guests tell about their high contacts and try to demoralize and influence the hoteliers.

Rules to tackle them are:

(i) Ignore their comments but don't ignore the guest.

(ii) Suggest alternatives, which would be better, and matches with guest status.

(iii) Be firm if the problem persists.

(c) CHATTER BOX GUESTS: They are generally old people or sometimes middle-aged females, which demands and expects respect from the senior persons of the hotel. The rule for them is to take the help of your colleagues in a right way eg. Phone call from the managers to the guest room.

(d) SOCIALIZER GUESTS: These guests try to be friendly with the hotel staff of opposite sex. The rule for them is to solve the humorous notes if still the problem persists, call the manager.

Status of rooms

Vacant Room: Vacant room is a room that has no defect and can be rented out. Vacant room also can be called a ready room or vacant

Ready room. Or OK room.

Arrival Room: This is a ready room, which has a definite booking. In this room you find drinking water, flower arrangement, fruit basket And bed side light on if it is an evening, (A.C. is on in addition to a vacant room) Also known as allocated room.

Occupied Room: This is a room, which has been occupied by a guest for one or more days. Housekeeping department has to service these Rooms daily.

Departure Room: This is a room from which the guest has checked out. It usually is in an untidy state. It is the responsibility of the

Housekeeping department to clean these rooms and make it ready for sale. Departure rooms are also known as check out rooms and vacant Dirty.

Out of Order Room (O.O.O): These rooms cannot be sold due to various defects Ex: A.C. not working, toilet cistern is not working,

Damp carper etc. It is the duty of the housekeeping department to inform the maintenance department to get them repaired as soon as Possible.

Day Let Room: These rooms are usually sold for people who come to stay during the daytime. The duration may be couple of hours. In Certain hotels these rooms are sold at a very low rate with limited facilities. In some hotels these rooms are given on complimentary basis Where the guests buy more than a certain number of tickets. The number of people who occupy these rooms is not restricted.

Held off Room :This term is used for a room which cannot be sold for a couple of hours for reasons such as interviews being held in it, or Used by artists for changing purposes, tailor working, or being used by hotel executives for inquiries, small meetings etc. This is usually Given on a complimentary basis.

Sleep Out Room: This is an occupied room where the guest has gone out of the room for few days, most probably on a tour. These rooms are kept double locked for security reasons and chambermaids carry out no routine cleaning. Normally no reduction is made on Accommodation charges.

Due out Room: This is an occupied room and the guest is expected to depart during the course of the day.

Front Office Systems

The technology used for front office record keeping and equipment has evolved and can mostly be found in three Stages. Properties may combine elements of each approach.

Non automated front office record keeping systems rely solely on handwritten forms. Reservations confirmations, Pre Registration and Occupancy forecasts are not common. Room assignments are made according to a room rack. The Registration card often doubles as a Room rack card and guest accounts folio. At departure, used registration cards Are filed in a box, as the hotel guest's history file.

A semi-automated front office system uses both hand written and machine produced forms. Pre registration activities Include preparation of registration cards, guest folios and information slips. During occupancy, cash registers and Posting machines are used to process many of the records formerly processed by hand. Desk agents are able to Quickly reconcile accounts and relay room status updates to the Housekeeping department.

Fully automated front office systems are computer based. The computer system may directly interface with a central reservation network and automatically block rooms, confirm reservations, perform pre-registration activities, and generate reports. Registration, room and account data are stored electronically in the computer for retrieval when needed. On-line credit card authorization terminals allow timely credit card approval. Guest charges are electronically transferred to the front desk and automatically posted. The system automatically creates a guest history record.

Qualities of Front Office Personnel

Since the front office is the most important department of the hotel as it generates the maximum revenue of the hotel. It is very essential for front office personnel to have qualities his qualities are:

1. Punctuality- he/she should be punctual in duty and should always report on time.
2. Has a positive attitude towards the job and the moral.
3. Recognizes both the positive and negative aspects of job.
4. Possess maturity in judgment
5. Should never be overfriendly with guests
6. Maintain control and composure ever in difficult situation.
7. Should be ever smiling.
8. Should exhibit cordial and pleasant nature.
9. Should have helpful attitude.
10. Should possess a good sense of humor.
11. Should practice good listening skills
12. Should be flexible in nature.
13. Should be well groomed in appearance
14. Good salesmanship.

<u>Grooming for Gentleman</u>

1. The hair should be clean, free from dandruff, odorless and glossy in appearance. It is necessary that all gentleman working in Front office should have short and neatly combed hair at all times i.e. not touching the ears and collars.
2. A clean daily shave is also compulsory. Always keep your mustaches well trimmed.
3. Hands carry germs, therefore, wash hands and nails frequently and always before leaving washroom.
4. Pay attention to your personal hygiene, use a deodorant to prevent body odor.
5. For those with bad smell can use mouthwash.
6. Wear clean, fresh and well-pressed uniforms at al times. Shirts and blazers should always be buttoned up.
7. Shoes should be nicely polished; heels should be of comfortable height and should always be black in color.
8. Wash face frequently if it l\tends to show up oil.

9. Do not wear a fancy jewellery, maximum being a ring and a watch.
10. Do not apply strong smelling perfumes / colognes / aftershave lotions. A mild fragrance is advisable.
11. It is compulsory to wear clear vests.
12. Always maintain an erect posture, slouching should be avoided.

Grooming for Ladies

1. Pay special attention to your hairstyle. Simple styles are desirable without the use of fancy hair clips.
2. For ladies with long hair, tying it up is mandatory.
3. Please be conservative in your use of cosmetics.
4. Use mouthwash to avoid mouth odor.
5. Keep hands clean and finger nails well manicured. Avoid the use of henna on hand.
6. Select a comfortable pair of footwear to match your uniform.
7. Pay special attention to your personal hygiene; apply deodorant rather than a heavy smelled perfume.
8. Wear fresh, clean and well-ironed uniform.
9. Drape (wear) your saree in conventional Indian style and not any other styles like gujrati etc.
10. Adopt a graceful posture and stand erect.

Front office forms

All properties must record certain information on the following forms (or their computer based equivalents) in order to operate efficiently.

A reservation record, detailing a reservation, enables the hotel to personalize service and schedule staff and facilities. A letter (or fax or email) of confirmation verifies that reservation has been made and that its specifications are accurate.

A reservations rack slip is used to monitor reservations.

A registration card contains guest personal data, length of stay, and method of settlement. In most countries, the guest's signature is required for the establishment of a legal relationship with the hotel. Printed statement relating to the storage of guest valuables may also be required.

A room rack slip contains guest personal data, room rate, expected departure date, and room number, and is placed in the room rack to indicate room status.

A guest folio is used to record the charges incurred and credits acquired by a guest during occupancy. Information from the guest registration card is transferred to the folio. Printed folios may have several duplicate pages, including one copy for the front office and one copy for the guest at check-out. Folio formats vary according to the front office record keeping system.

A voucher is a support document used to document information about a transaction. During the night audit, vouchers help ensure that transactions have been processed correctly.

Information rack slips, arranged alphabetically by guest name in the information rack, enable switchboard operators and guest services personnel to quickly determine the location of specific guests in the hotel.

A guest history record contains information relevant to marketing, sales, and servicing the guest's return. Law may require retention of certain data for some period of time.

An information rack lists guests alphabetically to assist front office employees with proper routing of telephone calls, mail and visitor inquiries.

A folio tray is used in none and semi automated properties to store guest folios. A fully automated front office may need a folio tray for temporary storage of folios printed for guests expected to depart.

A voucher rack stores vouchers for future reference.

FRONT OFFICE SALES MANSHIP

The difference between a successful hotel and an un-successful hotel is the ability of the staff to get a guest to spend an extra rupee and get the value for it. Most of the time a guest arrives to the hotel without an exact idea of how he is going to utilize his free time. A timely suggestion by the front office employee can stimulate a guest to utilize a service and pay for it. The front office staffs have a key role to play in hotel selling.

Following are the different aspects by which the quality to sell or we can say that the salesmanship of front office personnel can improve. In other words, the front office personnel should have the following qualities to be a good salesman.

1. PRODUCT KNOWLEDGE: Knowledge of the product is the most important quality, which front office personnel should have. He should be well dressed with the services offered by the hotel and types of rooms. The hotel has and should also possess detailed and correct information about the city. By the knowledge of the various products only, he would be able to sell them and can give suggestions to the guest to pass his free time. For eg. A very rich guest comes to the reception for a room for 02 nights. It is up to

the receptionist to understand the need and status of the guest. Receptionist may offer him the normal room with normal rates and on the same time, a good salesman at the reception can offer a high-class room by explaining to the guests about the extra services, which is offered in that particular room. To suggest same kind of services to the guest, knowledge of the product like knowledge of rooms and its types, knowledge of restaurant, other services hotel is offering etc.

2. SALES PROMOTION: Front office staff must be aware that the guest attaches value to the service sold and will be prepared to spend for it. For eg. a room has a maximum moderate and minimum rate attached to it. The maximum must be quoted but the value of the rate must be sold. The room may be overlooking the swimming pool or having a soft decor to please the guest.

After the room is allocated, the front office assistant may recommend a sauna bath and massage at the Health club especially after the guest has returned from a long journey. The assistant may volunteer to reserve his table at one of the restaurants and bar.

The good front office personnel always give the choice to the guest, so that guest should feel that he himself has make a final decision from the varieties opened to him.

3. GUEST NEEDS: A good salesman always understands the guest needs and thus recommend him the room or other kinds of services, which would therefore increase the sale. Any guest who has checked in the hotel has a motive or reason for that; it can be business, pleasure, fun, adventure etc. A good salesman would anticipate the guest needs and thus would do the suggestive selling accordingly. For eg. A guest arriving in the hotel for the purpose of business would be offered the facility like business center or board room, on the other hand, a guest arriving in the hotel for the purpose of relaxation would be offered services like spa, health club, swimming pool and the room should also be of the same standard.

4. DESIRE TO HELP: Desire to help the guest is an essential quality by which front office personnel can become a good salesman. A person should have desire in himself to help the guest is fulfilling his needs and expectations and should also give answers to all his queries.

5. COMMUNICATION: Communication holds the great importance for a person to become a good salesman. It's the way you communicate with guest leaves the impression of yourself and your nature in front of the guest. Things should be suggested to the guests to enhance the sale but it should

be in a way that guest should not feel defensive or he should not feels that things are forced upon him for the sake of money. For eg. Suggesting a presidential suite to a guest, front office assistant should use a very soft language like "May I suggest you" rather than using "You should go for presidential suite etc."

Here are some typical phrases to use:

"MAY I HELP YOU"

"MAY I RECOMMEND"

"I BEG YOUR PARDON"

"MAY I REQUEST YOU TO"

"ONE MOMENT PLEASE"

"WOULD YOU KINDLY"

CHAPTER THREE

Types of Lodging Facilities

Classification of hotel facilities is not based on rigid criteria. Definitions can change depending on market , legal criteria, location, function, and, in some cases, personal preference.

Hotels: A hotel usually offers guests a full range of accommodations and services, which may include reservations, suites, public dining and banquet facilities, lounge and entertainment areas, room service, cable television, personal computers, business services, meeting rooms, specialty shops, personal services, valet, laundry, hair care, swimming pool and other recreational activities, gaming/casino operations, ground transportation to and from an airport, and concierge services. The size of the property can range from 20 to more than 1000 rooms. Hotels are found in center city, suburban, and airport locations. Guest stays can be overnight or long term as long as several weeks. Properties sometimes specialize in catering to particular markets, such as conventions or gambling. Casino hotels usually take a secondary role to the casino operation, where the emphasis is on profitable gaming operations.

Motels: Motels offer guests a limited range of services, which may include reservations, vending machines, swimming pools, and setelite television. The size of these properties averages from 10 to 70 units. Motels are usually in suburban highway and airport locations. Guests typically stay overnight or for a few days. Motels may be located near a freestanding restaurant

All-suites: The all-suites concept was developed in the 80s as a separate marketing concept. These hotels offer guests a wide range of services that may include reservations, living room and separate bedroom, kitchenette, optional public dining room and room service, cable television, videocassette players and recorders, specialty shops, personal services, valet and laundry, swimming pool, and ground transportation to and from an airport. The size of the operation can range from 50 to more than 150 units. This type of property is usually found in center-city, suburban, and airport locations. The length of guest stay can be overnight, several days, or long term.

Select-service Hotels: Select-service hotels appeared in the mid 80s. The concept of select service was developed for a specific segment of the market: business and cost conscious travelers. The range of accommodations and services may include reservations, minimal public dining and meeting facilities, cable television, personal computers, personal services (valet and laundry), and ground transportation to and from an airport. The size of the property can range from 50 to more than 100 rooms. Select-service hotels are found in center-city, suburban, and airport locations. They are usually located near restaurants for guest convenience. Guest stays can be overnight or long term. These properties sometimes specialize in catering to the business traveler and offer special business technology centers.

Extended-stay: Hotels Extended-stay properties were designed to offer guests a home-away-from-home atmosphere over long stays precipitated by business, leisure, or personal necessity. For example, a person may have to attend to a business project for several days or weeks; another may want to visit with relatives whose home does not have adequate accommodations for visitors; a third may be accompanying a relative or friend receiving an extended health treatment at a medical center and require overnight accommodations.

RESORTS: Resorts may look like hotels or motor inns--the difference is that resorts most often are located at beaches or near the mountains. Resorts offer their guests recreational activities such as golf, horseback riding, tennis, and skiing. They may be chain or individually owned. Resorts may be open only "in season," though with the advent of indoor pools and big-named entertainment, many "summer" resorts are open year-round.

PRIVATELY OWNED HOUSING: Privately owned housing involves guest houses, condos, and time-shares.
It is becoming more common for people across the United States to "take in guests." Guest houses are privately owned homes where the owners rent individual bedrooms to visitors. Usually baths are shared with other guests or with the family.

Non-serviced accommodations: Non-serviced accommodation is a type of facility that provides tourists with accommodations without additional services. If you have non-serviced accommodations, guests at your facility cater for their housekeeping and catering costs. Examples of non-serviced types of accommodations you can invest in include cottages, caravans, and camping facilities.

Quality Ranking

Five Star Hotel – Outstanding, one of the best in the country. Exhibits an exceptionally high degree of service; striking, luxurious facilities with many extra amenities.

Four Star Hotel – Excellent, top-quality design and service. Displays a high level of service and hospitality. Properties offer a wide variety of amenities and upscale facilities inside the room, on the grounds, and in the common room areas.

Three Star Hotel – Offers a degree of sophistication. Additional amenities, services, and facilities may be offered.

Two Star Hotel – provides the bare essentials with some comfort quality. Standard (**)

One Star Hotel – offers only the essentials while meeting reasonable hygiene and security standards. Standard (*)

CHAPTER FOUR

THE RESERVATION PROCESS

The reservation process is of vital importance to a hotel because it gives the first impression of the hotel to guests.

1. Sells the main product of the hotel which is accommodation.

2. Generates customers for other departments.

3. Provides important management information to other departments.

The reservation process is often the first contact between a guest and the hotel. It is essential for the reservations clerk to provide prompt and accurate service in order to present a good first impression to the guest. Reservation information can be used by the hotel and by individual departments to:

1. Prepare sales forecasts.

2. Prepare weekly or monthly staff schedules, menus, and purchase requirements.

3. Relate sales forecasts to expenditure budgets.

4. Control costs including materials, labor and overheads.

5. Carry out long term planning (e.g., renovation of rooms and expansion programs).

6. Record reservation details accurately, in a manner which inspires your trust.

7. Be polite in their treatment.

8. A reservations agent must be well-trained in a number of areas: o reservation procedures

9. social skills (personal quality and interpersonal communication skills)

10. salesmanship (product knowledge and the ability to know how and what to sell)

TYPES OF RESERVATIONS

1. Guaranteed Reservation

• A guaranteed reservation means that a guest will guarantee to pay for the room even if it is not used, unless the guest has followed the hotel's prearranged cancellation procedure. In return, the hotel promises to hold the room until the check-out time of the day following the date of arrival.

• Guaranteed reservations protect the hotel from "no-shows" (guests who make a booking but do not arrive or cancel it). In this way the hotel will not lose the revenue from the room sales, should the guest not turn up.

• This system also protects the guest because the hotel agrees to ensure that a room will be kept for the guest, even if that guest arrives later than expected.

Reservations may be guaranteed in one of the following ways:

• Prepayment. The guest sends full payment for the room in advance.

• Credit card. The credit card number of the guest is recorded and if the guest fails to turn up, the hotel will bill the card holder in the normal way. This is the most common form of guaranteed reservation.

• Advance deposit (or partial prepayment). The guest sends a specified amount of money in advance (normally to cover one night's accommodation). This form of deposit is usually required for group booking or long-stay guests. If the guest fails to show or cancels their booking, the prepayment may be retained by the hotel or returned to the guest or company depending on the hotel policy

• Contractual agreement. This normally involves a corporation where the company has agreed with the hotel to pay for an agreed number of rooms regardless of whether or not they are used.

2. Non-Guaranteed Reservation

A non-guaranteed reservation is a reservation in which the guest has simply agreed and confirmed that they will arrive. It is normal with this type of reservation for the hotel to agree to hold a non-guaranteed room until a stated cancellation time, normally up to 6:00 PM on the day of

• Type and number of rooms required

• number of persons

Sources of Reservation

Sources are the different people or organizations that make reservations, such as:

1. Individual Guests who independently make reservations with the hotel on their own.

2. Travel Agents include travel agencies who make reservation on behalf of guests who are travelling on tour packages.

3. Companies who have separate travel departments who make their booking when they travel for official work.

4. Hotel Sales & Marketing Executives include staff of the hotel that approaches various business Houses. They try to sell the services offered by the hotel.

Procedure for Individual Reservation

1. The hotel first receives the reservation request from the guest either through telephone, letter or personally.

2. The reservation assistant asks about the arrival and departure dates of the guest. Then information about the type of room and number of rooms is asked.

3. The reservation assistant matches the reservation request of the guest with the room availability with the help of a computerized booking system.

4. If the request does not match with room availability, other dates or types of rooms are offered to the guest.

5. In case the request matches the room availability, the processing of the reservation is done by finding out other information from the guest. This includes name of the guest, position, company or home address, time and arrival details, billing details and any other special information. This information is recorded in the reservation form.

6. Finally, the reservation assistant gives a confirmation number to the guests, which is proof of the confirmation by the hotel

Procedure for Group Reservation

1. Firstly, the hotel receives the reservation request from the group either through a group leader or by personal meeting or some other mode.

2. The reservation assistant asks about the arrival and departure dates of the group. Then information about the type of room and number of rooms is asked.

3. The reservation assistant matches the reservation request of the guests with the room availability and with the help of a computerized booking system.

4. If the request does not match with room availability, other dates or types of rooms are offered to the group.

5. In case the request matches the room availability, the reservation assistant discusses with group leader about the number of rooms to be kept aside for the group and also the cut-off dates i.e. the last date till which the

hotel will reserve the rooms for the group.

6. The reservation assistant then starts processing the reservation request and takes other details such as name of the group, name of the group leader and group members, number and type of guest rooms required, date and time of arrival of the group, date and time of departure of the group, meal plans, billing details and any other special information.

7. Finally, the reservation assistant gives a confirmation number to the group leader and then sends the confirmation letter.

BASIC RESERVATION ACTIVITIES

1. Receiving Inquiries: The first step in the reservation process is to obtain information about a guest's proposed stay, to check whether a room is available.

The information a reservations agent needs to obtain from the guest in order to give a speedy response, is as follows:

- Date of arrival
- Length of proposed stay
- Type and number of rooms required
- Number of persons

2. Determining room availability: After obtaining the information about the proposed stay of the guest, the next step is to find out if the room(s) required is available. In any reservation system, it is essential to keep a close check on the number of reservations taken to avoid excessive overbooking. Overbooking occurs when a hotel accepts more bookings than the number of rooms which are available. By overbooking, the hotel may find that they have major problems and loss of goodwill at hand.

Note that it is common in many hotels for the reservations department to overbook intentionally in order to ensure that a full house (100% occupancy) will be achieved. The practice of overbooking helps to reduce the loss in revenue due to no-shows and late cancellations.

Whether hotels intentionally overbook or not, an effective system has to be used to check on room availability. This can be accomplished through the use of:

- Forecast boards
- Reservation charts
- Computerized systems

3. Accepting or Denying Requests for Reservations: Having checked that a room is available, the reservations agent will either accept or deny a booking.

If a room is available, the request will normally be accepted. The reservations agent will then record the details onto a reservations form or a computer terminal.

The reservations department may choose not to accept a booking (this is called denying a booking). Denying a booking happens when:

• A hotel may not have the specified accommodation available on the requested date(s).

• A hotel is fully booked.

• A guest is known to be on the blacklist. (A blacklist is a record authorized by the hotel management of the names of persons not welcome in the hotel for various reasons.)

When denying a specific reservation request, the reservation agent should always be polite and helpful, and should follow this procedure:

If the specific accommodation required is not available: Apologize to the guest and explain that the particular accommodation requested is not available. Try to help by offering alternative accommodation or dates at the hotel, or in a sister hotel.

If the hotel is fully booked: Apologize and explain that the hotel is fully booked. Offer alternative dates or accommodation at the hotel or in another hotel of the group. Cumulative historical data of all denied bookings should be kept.

If the guest is blacklisted: The actions to follow will depend on the reasons why the guest was blacklisted. For example, the reservation clerk may refuse the request completely if the guest has previously been a nuisance, or accept the request but on a cash-only basis if the guest is known to be bad in settling bills. Complicated cases should be referred to the Front Office Manager.

4. Documenting reservation details: If the request for a reservation is accepted, the reservations agent will then complete a reservation form, recording all the necessary details concerning the guest and their stay. It is essential for the reservations agent to ask if the guest has stayed in the hotel previously. In a computerized system, this will immediately link a returnee guest to their profile which will give the hotel insights on the guest's preferences and status (e.g. VIP status, number stays in the hotel, special requests, etc.)

The reservation form is the only document which contains all the relevant information about the prospective guest and their accommodation request. It is very important that the form is fully and accurately completed.

When obtaining the reservation details from the guest, the reservations agent should also explain the differences between a guaranteed and non-guaranteed booking. Should a guest decide to guarantee their booking, the reservations agent has to obtain additional information concerning the method of guarantee (e.g. credit card, prepayment, or deposit).

Once a request has been accepted and the details of the reservation recorded, the reservations clerk must immediately update the room availability chart. This ensures that the room availability record is accurate and thereby helps to avoid overbooking or commissions.

Guest Profile

a. The details recorded in the guest profile could easily be retrieved upon opening the guest's reservation in the computer system. The guest's profile should include the following:

- guest's name
- type of accommodation requestcd
- length of stay
- rate and terms quoted
- how and when booked
- contact numbers
- reservation agent's initials
- remarks

b. A guest profile could specially be advantageous to repeat guests. This allows both the reservations and the front desk agents to detect guest preferences by referring to their previous reservations.

c. The remarks section would usually list the preferences of the guest. If there are particular services that should be prepared prior to the guest's arrival, this would automatically be printed on the trace report which serves as a reminder to the front office of what to do on the arrival date of the guest.

5. Confirming reservations

- Confirmation of a reservation is a written acknowledgement sent by the hotel to the guest.

- It confirms that a request for a room has been made with the hotel, and is written evidence that a contract has been made between a hotel and a prospective guest.

• As part of the confirmation process, the computer system automatically assigns a reservation confirmation number to each booking.

6. Maintaining reservation records: Occasionally, a change to or cancellation of a booking is requested. In these cases, an amendment or cancellation form is completed by the reservations agent and attached to the original reservation form and correspondence.

At the same time, the room availability chart should be amended accordingly In the case of a booking cancellation, various details are recorded to ensure that the correct booking is cancelled. It is also necessary to show who is responsible for canceling the booking, i.e. who in the hotel received the cancellation and who on behalf of the guest made the cancellation.

The cancellation details should include:

• date of original booking

• guest's name

• date of cancellation

• name of person who cancelled the booking

• cancellation number

• name of reservations agent who received the cancellation – as with denied bookings, all the details of guaranteed or non- guaranteed.

7. Compiling reservation reports

• Expected arrivals and expected departures list. Lists of guests who are due to arrive or depart on a particular day.

• Room availability report. A list showing both the number of rooms sold and are available.

• Group status report. A list of groups due to arrive/depart, with information on the group size and whether their bookings are

• Special arrivals list. List of special guests, VIPs, or guests with special requests.

• Turn-away report. A report on the number of reservations denied.

• Revenue forecast report. A report of projected revenue from future room sales.

• Trace report. A list of the guest's preference(s) and special request(s) that should be prepared prior to the guest's arrival.

CHECK-IN PROCEDURE

Guests have often traveled a long way and may be impatient and tired when they arrive at a hotel. They will, therefore, want quick, efficient check-in services provided by pleasant and courteous receptionists. To a hotel, arrival is the occasion when guest and hotel staffs meet face-to-face for the first time. A well-functioning reception process gives the guest a good impression of the hotel. This helps to establish the hotel's image and reputation, as well as to encourage the guest to return in the future. In order to give guests a lasting first impression, the reception staff needs to be efficient and have good social skills.

They should be knowledgeable about the accommodation product of their hotel and skilled in the check-in procedures, and the handling of guests' queries. Additionally, they should have pleasant manners, be cordial, empathetic, and always be ready to help. A neat and tidy appearance and the ability to communicate with guests are also essential.

Checklist for welcoming the guest

The following checklist may give you some idea of the appropriate social skills necessary when dealing with guests:

1. Maintain good eye contact; eye contact is very important because it shows attention and respect. However, do be careful not to turn your eye contact in a stare. It is also worth noting that positive eye contact is not regarded as courteous by the people of many Asian countries, especially Japan.

2. Smile when talking to the guest; it shows a warm and the reception department is often the first hotel positive manner

a. Stand up straight and avoid leaning or slouching. The way you stand is important; standing straight shows respect and attention. Leaning on the front desk, on the other hand, suggests that the receptionist is tired, and cannot be bothered.

3. Maintain a clean, neat and tidy personal appearance at all times. By paying attention to your dress and personal hygiene, you show that you have a pride in yourself and your hotel

4. Speak clearly, using a pleasant tone. In this way, the guest will easily understand what you say and be impressed by your courtesy.

Basic Check-in Activities

The process of checking in new arrivals can be divided into five basic stages. However, you should note that the order of these stages may vary from hotel to hotel. The reservation status of the guest may pre-empt some of the stages. For example, a VIP guest would normally have their room pre-allocated, and might well register in the room or suite.

Preparation for guest arrival

Before the actual registering of a guest or assigning a room, the receptionists need to have at hand certain information which is essential in their work. Such information should include:

- room status and availability
- expected arrivals and departures
- arrivals with special requests
- VIPs and frequent-stay guests

Much of this information is determined the night before the day of arrivals. However, in hotels with computerized systems this information is updated with every room transaction. It is also permanently at hand and can be easily accessed through the keyboard.

The following are check-in activities perform in the front office attendant;

1. Preparation for guest arrival
2. Room assignment and determination of room rate
3. Registration
4. Checking the method of payment
5. Issuing the room key and escorting the guest

The room status report and assignment

Before the guests arrive, reception staff will need details on the status of the guest- rooms. This information is usually indicated if a room is occupied, vacant and dirty, ready for occupancy or out of order. From a room status report, reception staff will be able to identify which rooms are clean and ready for guests, which rooms will become available later in the day, or which rooms are unavailable on that date. Such information is essential to the reception department when assigning rooms, to ensure that a guest is not inconvenienced by being sent to an occupied, dirty or faulty room.

Room Status Classification:

• Occupied/stay-on rooms. These are rooms still occupied by guests, who will stay on for one or more

• Vacant/clean. The rooms have been vacated and serviced, and are ready to be assigned to a guest.

• Vacant/dirty. The rooms have recently been vacated and waiting for cleaning. Normally, it will take at least 30 minutes for housekeeping to prepare these rooms.

• Departure rooms. These rooms are not in use, usually because there is something which is faulty in the room, or the room is being re-decorated.

• Blocked rooms. These are rooms reserved for specific reasons (e.g. for VIPs or tours or because of their location).

• In-house-used. These are rooms used by the hotel's manager or upper position the organizations.

Expected Arrival List

The expected arrivals list provides basic information on guests who are expected to arrive on a particular date. Regardless of whether this information is given by computer or manually, the details should be the same. By checking the expected arrivals against the room status report, the reception supervisor will be able to determine:

• Whether there are sufficient rooms to accommodate all the guests expected to arrive.

• The number of rooms that will be available for accommodating any walk-in guests.

If it is found that there are insufficient rooms to accommodate all expected arrivals on that date (i.e. when there is overbooking), the reception supervisor may have to seek additional accommodation in nearby hotels. This process of having to book an expected arrival into another hotel because you are full is sometimes called walking the guest. In most cases, the original hotel will pay for the transportation to and from the other hotel as well as any excess room charges.

The Guest History Record

Most professional hotels keep guest history records which contain details on all previous guests. With the advent of computerization, this information is now easily made available to all hotels that use computers. If a guest history record is available, the names of all the guests on the expected arrivals list should be checked against the guest history record to see if any of the guests have previously stayed in the hotel A check should also be made to ascertain what appropriate action should be taken to ensure that they will enjoy their stay. For example, if a guest has previously complained of a noisy room, the reception supervisor may assign a room on a floor away from the noise.

If a frequent-stay guest had been previously upgraded to a better room, but on this occasion the hotel is unable to upgrade the guest, then extra amenities, like a fruit basket, may be placed in the room. A VIP or a frequent-stay guest should be greeted on arrival by the front office manager or guest relations officer. In some cases, the guest may be met by the general manager .

Expected arrivals with special requests

Some guests may request extra amenities or services when they make their reservations. The relevant departments must, therefore, be informed of these requests so that they can be prepared and are ready for the guests' arrival.

For example, if an expected guest has requested a cot for a baby, the reception supervisor will assign a suitable room number for the reservation, and inform the housekeeper of the request for a cot. The housekeeper will then place the cot and any other items, such as a baby basket containing talcum powder, in the room before the guest arrives.

List of Important Guests Most hotels pay special attention to important guests. Important guests may include:

• VIPs (very important persons), e.g. frequent guests, celebrities, guests in expensive rooms, guests with security risks, executives from the hotel's head office, and so on.

• CIPs (commercially important persons). May be guests and executives of large corporate account-holders, important journalist and media staff, travel agents and tour company staff, and guests whose companies could bring a lot of business to the hotel in the future.

• SPATTs (special attention guests) are guests who may need extra care and attention, such as handicapped guests, elderly or ill guests, and long-stay guests. These important guests tend to be given special services or amenities during their stay. Such services may include the assignment of the guest's room before they arrive; the complimentary use of the hotel transport; registration in their room; and being greeted and escorted by special staff when they arrive. In order to alert staff of the arrival of important guests, a list of important guests is produced and sent to other sections of the front office and to all other operating departments.

Other preparations for guest arrivals

In addition to collecting information for check-in, receptionists may carry out other preparatory work before guests arrive at a hotel. The preparation of registration documents before guest arrivals can greatly reduce the time and work at check-in, thus speeding up the process during the busy hours.

Some computer systems can pre-print the registration cards for the expected arrivals. This means that some of the personal details of the expected guests are printed on the registration card, e.g. name, address, dates of arrival and departure, and method of payment. When the guests arrive, all they then have to do is to check these details and sign the registration card.

REGISTRATION

The purpose of registration is to record a guest's arrival and confirm their personal details, as well as to satisfy legal requirements. It is not legally necessary for the visitor to sign the registration document nor is it necessary for them to give them the information in person; it can be done through a third party and either orally or in writing. However, most hotels expect much more information and certainly a signature, as you will see in the section on the registration form.

When a guest arrives at a hotel, he or she is normally required to complete a registration form. There may be differences in the reservation status of newly arrived guests, and they will, therefore, be dealt with differently at the time of registration.

• Guests with reservations For a guest with a reservation, the process of registration and room allocation occurs Immediately on arrival. The receptionist will ask the guest to complete and sign a registration form and will check these details against the details held at reception.

Should there be any discrepancies, it needs to be clarified at this point.

• Walk-in guests If the guest is a walk-in, then the receptionist must first check the room availability before registering the guest. If a room is available, it will be offered, and the guest must be informed of all room charges. Upon acceptance, the guest will be asked to complete a registration form.

The Registration Form

A registration form or card is used to record the personal particulars of the guest on arrival. The actual design or layout of the forms may vary among hotels, but they usually ask for similar guest information.

a. Arrival date. The arrival date is obtained from the reservation record and may be written or printed in the space provided in the form.

b. Departure date. The departure date will be transferred, in the same manner as the arrival date, from the reservation record, and written or printed in the form. This detail must be confirmed by the receptionist at check-in.

c. Arrival time. The actual arrival time section will be completed by reception at the time of check-in.

d. Number of rooms. Information on the number of rooms is transferred from the reservation file and confirmed with guest.

e. Room type. Information on the room type is transferred from the reservation file, and must be confirmed by the receptionist at check-in. It is possible for the guest to be upgraded, or be assigned on another type of accommodation depending on the agreement at check-in.

f. Daily rate. If a guest has made a reservation prior to arrival, the daily room rate information will be transferred from the reservation file. For a walk-in guest, this has to be determined at the time of room assignment.

g. Number of guests. Information on the number of guests is transferred from the reservation file. It should be noted that the number of guests may not be the same as the number of beds in the accommodation. For example, one guest may be staying in a twin room on a single occupancy rate, or three guests may be staying in a suite or in a twin room with an extra bed.

h. Advance deposit. If an advance deposit has been paid, the amount of the deposit will be recorded. The details of the deposit will be transferred from the reservation file onto the registration form. The receptionist may then confirm them receipt of the deposit with the guest on arrival. The amount of deposit received will then be transferred from the advance deposit account to the guest folio.

i. Room number. Before printing out the registration form, the receptionist will assign a room to the guest. The room number will then be recorded on the registration form.

j. Package plan. The type of package or tariff to be paid by the guest will be printed in the form. The guest may be staying on 'room-only' terms, or 'bed and breakfast', or as part of a 'tour' package which includes some meals, or as a conference' delegate where meals, room, function room facilities and entertainments are all included in the plan.

k. Name. The guest's surname, first name and title are transferred from the reservation record. It is very important for the receptionist to check that the guest's name is spelled correctly.

l. Address. If the guest is to have their bill settled by a company, it is most likely that the company address will be transferred from the reservation record. Also, if the reservation was made by a travel agent, the agent's address will have been previously recorded. If the guest is to settle their own account, then the residential address should be recorded. It is useful to have the guest's residential address as well as business address. The residential address is needed to enable the hotel to forward any mail or contact the guest after departure; the company address may be used for marketing purposes.

m. Passport number and date and place of issue. If the guest is an alien, they must provide their passport number at check-in. The receptionist may have to request to see the guest's passport, and check the details.

n. Nationality. By law, the nationality of a guest must be recorded. If the guest has stayed beforc, this detail may be automatically transferred from the guest history record.

o. Company name. If the guest is to have the bill settled by their company, the name of the company should be checked against the approved company list prepared by the sales office or credit controller. If the booking was made by a travel agent, the agent's name may be transferred from the travel agent's file.

p. Payment by. The method of payment should be transferred from the reservation file. This information is very important to the hotel and care must be taken in confirming this with the guest.

q. Departing to. If this detail has been recorded at the time of reservation, then it will be transferred from the reservation file. If the information is not available in the reservation record, the receptionist should ask the guest where they plan to travel next.

This information is of interests to hotel because, should the guest be traveling to a city where the hotel group has another hotel, then the receptionist can suggest an onward booking.

r. Signature. It is important to ensure that the guest reads the details before signing in the registration card. By signing the card, the guest acknowledges the terms and conditions of the hotel operation

s. Receptionist signature. It is important that the reception clerk signs the registration form.

Should any queries arise in the future regarding the guest, or any of the guest's details, then the hotel immediately knows whom to ask for further information, or clarification.

t. Signature. It is important to ensure that the guest reads the details before signing in the registration card. By signing the card, the guest acknowledges the terms and conditions of the hotel operation Policy statements. Many hotels print the policy statements of the hotel at the bottom of the registration card. This is an opportunity to ensure that the guest is aware of such policies.

The Blacklist

Some hotels have a blacklist, which is a list of the names of people who are not welcome at the hotel, e.g. rowdy persons, people who have not settled their previous accounts, and undesirable personality. The list can be compiled using information from:

a. police reports

b. the reports from other local hotels

c. the corporate office

d. the assistant manager's log book

e. accounts department or credit manager

This list must be tightly controlled by the front office manager, and problems arising from the use of the list should be referred to this manager

Pre-arrival registration

One of the busiest times for the reception department is during the check-in hours. To ensure that newly arrived guests are greeted and given their rooms as smoothly and efficiently as possible, speedy registration procedures are required.

One way is to pre-print all of the guest's details on a registration card prior to their arrival, as previously mentioned. All the guest then has to do is check that the details are correct, sign the card and receive their room key.

Pre-registration can also be the solution to checking in large numbers of guests simultaneously, e.g. groups, tours or conference delegates.

Room Assignment and Room Rate

The process of assigning rooms and room rates differs with the different categories of guests.

a. Expected arrivals- The room rate for expected arrivals (i.e. guests with reservations) is agreed by the guest when the reservation is made, and rooms are not normally assigned until the guest arrives at the hotel.

However, this does not apply if the guest wants a specific room, or has made a special request, e.g. for a bed board or cot, or if the guest is a VIP or CIP. In such cases rooms are pre-allocated.

b. Walk-in guests-Walk-in guests can only be assigned rooms and room rates after it has been confirmed that there is accommodation available. It is normal for the cost of at least one night's accommodation to be asked for in advance of the guest's stay.

This order provides for the display of the maximum and minimum current prices charged per night for accommodation.

Examples of accommodation prices when must be displayed are:

• the price of a bedroom for one person, e.g. INR-5000.00 per night or INT-4000.00- INR-5 000.00 when there is a range of prices

  • the price of a bedroom for two persons

  • the price of a bed in any other type of room But:

• If the prices include GST, this must be stated, e.g. INR-5000.00 per night, including GST.

• If there is a service charge, it must be included in the price, e.g. INR-6000.00 per night, including GST and service charge.

• If the guest has to pay for meals as part of the charge for accommodation, this must be stated, e.g. INR-50,00.00 per night, including breakfast, GST and service charge.

Types of Room Rates

Hotels have developed various room rate categories to attract different markets. These rates will depend on seasons, number of potential sales in a market, and other factors.

a. Rack Rate – the highest room rate charged by a hotel, is the rate given to a guest who does not fall into any particular category, such as a walk-in who requests a room for the night.

b. Corporate Rate – it is a rate offered to businesspeople staying in the hotel.

c. Commercial Rate – are room rates for businesspeople that represent a company and have infrequent or sporadic patterns of travel.

d. Military and Educational Rate –room rates that are established for military personnel and educators.

e. Group Rate –room rates that are offered to large groups of people visiting the hotel.

f. Family Rate – rates offered to encourage visits by families with children.

g. Package Rate – room rates that include goods and services in addition to rental of a room. It is developed by marketing and sales department to lure guests into a hotel during low sales periods.

h. Complimentary Rate – a rate for which there is no charge to the guest.

These rate categories have variations in all hotels. The purpose of the rate categories is to attract groups of guests who will supply repeat business and help ensure full occupancy.

Room Assignment

When assigning a room to a specific guest, the receptionist has to ensure, as much as possible, that the needs and preferences of the guest are satisfied. The receptionist, in order to do his/her job better, needs to know the following:

a. The status of all the rooms in the hotel.

b. The position and features of each room in the hotel.

c. The needs, preference and/or special requests of the guest.

Information on room status will be obtained from the room status board or report, while the guest's needs and preferences can be obtained from the expected arrivals, and the special requests/VIP lists. The position and facilities of each room are usually indicated by a floor plan.

Room assignment by computer

In modern hotels, room assignment is often done by computer. When the receptionist enters the required room type and the requested period of stay into the computer, it will automatically display several suitable alternatives on the screen. It is then up to the receptionist to choose the most suitable room by using their knowledge of the facilities of the rooms (e.g. their view, floor and features), and comparing it with the details on the reservation (room type or special requests).

The receptionist may also refer to the guest history record for the personal preferences of that guest. Each time a receptionist checks-in a guest into a vacant room, the computer will change its record of the room status from vacant to occupy. This ensures that the room availability is continually updated.

Early check-ins

On occasion, a guest may arrive earlier than expected and there may be no vacant or clean rooms available. In such circumstances there are a variety of options that the receptionist can take.

Check to see if there is an alternative type of room that is vacant/clean and offer that to the guest, e.g. a twin instead of a double.

• If an alternative is not available, apologize to the guest and explain that their room has not yet been vacated and/or cleaned.

• Register the guest, but do not assign a room until a suitable vacant/clean room is available.

• Have a guest's luggage put into store until a room can be assigned. Then have it taken up to the room.

• The guest should be given a time when they can return to

• collect the room key. Alternatively, a note should be made of the guest's whereabouts, so that they may be contacted as soon as the room is ready.

• Contact housekeeping to rush the room (i.e. telephone the housekeeper to give a particular room priority on their cleaning schedule)

It is important to make sure that all staff members on the reception desk are made aware that there is a guest waiting for a room. This is especially true when one reception shift hands over to another. Reception staff must also realize that guests may get every impatient if they cannot go straight to their rooms.

The receptionist should be very empathetic, and make every effort to ensure that the guests feel comfortable while waiting. For example, the receptionist may inform the guests of the location of the bar and coffee shop, beach, promenade or children's play area, so that the guest can fill in time while they are waiting.

Checking the Method of Payment

When a guest makes a reservation, their intended method of payment is recorded. However, it is important to confirm the method of payment at the time of the guest's arrival.

The main reason for doing this is to ensure that the hotel can know in advance if the guest needs to make special arrangements for settling their bill, e.g. wanting to pay by check, or to use uncommon foreign currency.

This precaution helps to prevent embarrassment to the guest at check out, as well as preventing walk-outs. A walk-out occurs when a guest leaves without checking out and paying their bill.

General rules for checking the method of payment

• If the guest is a walk-in or has a non-guaranteed reservation, take a pre-payment or a credit card imprint.

• If the guest has a guaranteed reservation and is settling their own account, ask to take a credit card imprint, and phone for authorization for an amount which is estimated to cover the whole stay.

• If the guest wants to pay by cash or foreign currency, inform them of the room rate and record the method of payment on the record card. Confirm with the guest that the rates for the foreign currency are as displayed.

For settlements by check, ensure that the check guarantee card will cover the whole amount. Remember that it contravenes the check card agreement to use multiple checks for settlement of one bill.

• When a guest has a company or travel agent who is settling the account, the receptionist must ensure that accurate billing details are recorded, e.g. what is paid by the company or agent and what expenses are the guest's own responsibility.

Advance deposits: Some guests may have sent an advance deposit to guarantee their reservation. The receptionist should confirm that the deposit has been received while the guest is checking in. A credit is then immediately indicated to the guest's bill.

Paying by credit card: If a guest is to settle all or part of the account by credit card, it is common procedure to request an imprint of the card at check-in. this allows the hotel time to check whether or not the card is valid.

If a guest wants to settle their account using a credit card which the hotel does not accept, then they must be immediately informed so that an alternative method of settlement can be arranged.

The Key Card: After registration and room assignment, a guest is issued a key to the room. It is common practice to give a key card, together with the key, to the guest.

The key card is a personal record to the guest's room number and room rate, and a statement of the hotel's policies. It also serves as proof of the guest's identity to hotel staff. This may be necessary when the guest wants to collect the room key from reception or sign for a drink or meal.

The practice of escorting guests to their rooms depends on the standard service offered by a hotel. In most budget hotels and motels, guests are not normally escorted to their rooms. Instead, they are given directions and may have to carry their own bags.

On the other hand, full-service hotels usually offer a bell service. The bellboys frequently escort guests to their rooms and at the same time handle their baggage. In top-class hotels, where there are a large number of staff at the reception, the receptionist who checks in a guest may escort them to the room, and the bellboys will deliver the luggage shortly afterwards.

The purpose of this attentive service is to show the guest that the hotel considers them important. The escorting staff will spend time explaining the facilities and services of the room, answering questions, and trying to make the guest feel welcome.

Some hotels employ guest relations officers (GROs) who greet VIPs and frequent-stay guests and personally escort them to their rooms immediately on arrival.

In these situations, the room will have been assigned and the key card and key prepared before the guest arrives. As soon as the guest walks through the hotel entrance they are escorted to the room, where the GRO carries out the registration procedure. In this way, an important guest does not have to wait in the busy front office area for check-in.

This is a particularly important service for those guests who wish full anonymity or who, for security reasons, do not want to linger in a public place.

The Check- in Process

So far, we have described the various activities during the process of checking in new arrivals.

Developing your Check- in Skills

In the previous lesson, we explained the duties of the receptionist in welcoming guests and checking in new arrivals. A good receptionist should have, in addition to a full understanding of the reception duties; good social skills and be well trained in the operational procedures of the reception department.

In this section, we shall try to help develop such skills by giving some examples of interactions between the guest and the receptionist during check-in. Through these activities, we hope that students can:

• Develop the appropriate vocabulary and phrases.

• Adopt an appropriate manner and style of speech.

• Better understand the operational procedures involved in checking in guests.

Key points:

1. All guests should be treated with equal respect, courtesy, and attention, regardless of their status. Always extend a warm welcome, and a cheerful greeting.

2. The front desk clerk asked the guest for his name and initial and then checked against the arrivals list for that day.

3. A telephone message was taken before the guest arrived. The message was sent to the reception department, and was noted on the arrivals list so that when the guest checked in the message could be immediately given to the guest.

4. The front desk clerk can ask the guest to complete the front desk registration form or, as an additional service, the front desk clerk can complete the registration card for the guest. The guest is then asked to sign the registration card.

5. No mention was made of this reservation being guaranteed, so the front desk clerk must ask how the account will be settled. Settlement may be secured by taking a credit card imprint or by the guest paying cash in advance. Mr. Brothers wants to settle by credit card.

6. Mr. Brothers also requested information on safe deposits. The front desk clerk offered to help him and did not immediately refer him to the cashier. Reception department staff should try to give immediate personal service when handling enquiries; this gives the guest a greater sense of belonging and importance.

7. The registration card, corresponding and credit card imprint may be given to a cashier. The cashier will check the credit card number against the special bulletin of void cards supplied by Visa, and open an account in the guest's name. However, this part of the check-in procedure is very often performed by reception.

Overbooking

It has been previously mentioned that 'overbooking' is the accepting of more reservations than there are rooms available, and is a standard practice in most hotels. This is done to compensate for the percentage of no-shows, cancellations and late departures which regularly occur. Customers who cancel their bookings at the last minute, or simply do not show up on the expected day of arrival, cost the hotel a large amount of money because a room is being held for them, and the hotel does not receive the revenue because they do not arrive. Therefore, to achieve a full house and revenue it is necessary for hotels to adopt an overbooking policy. To be able to implement an accurate overbooking procedure the front office manager and reservations clerk need to have all the relevant historical data on the percentage of no-shows, guaranteed and non-guaranteed bookings, cancellations and early departures. With this information, management should be able to predict the overbooking percentage rates based on those figures.

Additional information which is also important in achieving accurate overbooking figures is the possible number of walk-ins, the present reservations status, and the special events and functions which are happening in the hotel or surrounding area.

The greater the information available for the front office manager, the more accurately the overbooking can be forecasted. Many hotel companies now use computer systems in which to record all the relevant data, making it much easier to forecast the hotel's overbooking. Overbooking is typical of transient or city center hotels, which have a higher incidence of no-shows, cancellations and early departures. In order to maintain an accurate and up-to-date room availability record, good communication is required between reservations and the front desk, as well as the sales department.

For example, if a guest wishes to extend their stay, this should be communicated to the reservations department, so that the availability chart can be updated. Overbooking is also one of the basic strategies employed in yield/revenue management. Occasionally, front office management may predict the wrong levels of overbooking. Consequently, the hotel finds that it is responsible for 'walking a guest'. 'Walking a guest' means turning away a guest who holds a reservation, owing to the lack of available rooms. Because the hotel is in breach of contract by not having a room available for the guest, every attempt should be made to mitigate the financial compensation that an irate customer might claim through legal action. This may be done by locating the guest at another hotel of the same or of better standard, paying for transportation costs to the other hotel, and paying for any meals which may be included in the original hotel package and any increased room charge at the alternative hotel.

Despite all of these minimum measures, the hotel guest can still sue for breach of contract, and the inconvenience which it has caused. If the receptionist finds that overbooking has occurred, a procedure to be followed prior to the guest's arrival could be:

• Anticipate early in the day by how many rooms the hotel will be overbooked.

• Check the arrivals list against room status, checking for non-guaranteed, guaranteed, release time and possible no shows. This indicates the number of people who possibly may not arrive, as well as anticipating how many guests will have to be 'walked'.

• Check the bed occupancy list against room status; this will indicate how many stay-ons, stay-overs and late departures there may be for that particular day. \o Check with the housekeeper if any 'OO'/'OOO' (out of order) rooms can be made available.

• Check for company bookings, to ensure that they are guaranteed arrivals.

It is possible for two regular business people to share? (Possibly offer discount

or complimentary gift.)

• Reserve the necessary rooms in another hotel in the immediate area.

• If possible, book out only one-night stays.

• Check who to 'walk' – tourist or business person?

• Arrange transportation for guests to the new hotel.

• Inform the telephone operator of the guest's alternative hotel.

• Ensure that reception personnel and front office management are kept informed of all overbooking developments, especially at the changeover of shifts.

• Notify the general manager of the overbooking situation, in case of any future repercussions.

• Ensure that the duty manager is fully aware of the situation.

CHAPTER SIX

Guest Cycle

The guest cycle: The financial transactions of the guest makes while staying in the hotel determine the flow of business through the property. Traditionally flow of cycle can be divided into a four-stage

PRE ARRIVAL: The guest chooses a hotel during the pre arrival stage of the guest cycle. The guests choice can be affected by many factors, including previous experiences with the hotel: advertisements, company travel policy, recommendations from travel agents, friends, or business associates, the hotels location or reputation, frequent traveler programmes, preconceptions based upon the hotel's name or chain affiliation. The guest's decision may also be influenced by the ease of making reservations and how the reservations agent describes the hotel and its facilities, room rates and amenities. The reservation department employees should be <sales oriented= and present a positive strong image of the hotel. The attitude, efficiency, and knowledge of the front office staff may influence a caller's decision to stay at a particular hotel.

A reservations agent must be able to respond quickly and accurately to request for future accommodations. The proper handling of reservation information can be critical to the success of lodging property. Efficient procedures will also allow more time for the reservations agent to capture needed information and to market hotel services.

If a reservation can be accepted as requested, the reservations agent creates a reservation record .the creation of reservation record initiates the hotel guest cycle. The record enables the hotel to personalize guest service and appropriately schedule needed staff and facilities. By confirming reservation the hotel verifies a guest's room request and personal information, and assures the guest that his or her needs will be addressed. Using the information collected during the reservation process, a hotel may also be able to complete pre registration activities. Such activities include assigning a specific room and rate to guests who have not yet registered and preparing a guest folio. A guest folio is a record of the charges incurred and credits acquired by the guest during occupancy.

An effective reservation system helps maximize room sales by accurately monitoring room availabilities and forecasting room revenue. By analyzing reservation information, front office management can develop an understanding of the hotel's reservation patterns. Data collected during reservation process becomes useful in subsequent front office functions. The most important outcome of an effective reservations process is having a room available when the guest arrives.

ARRIVAL: The arrival stage of the guest cycle includes registration and rooming functions. After the guest arrives, he or she establishes a business relationship with the hotel through the front office. It is front office staff's responsibility to clarify the nature of the guest-hotel relationship and to monitor the financial transactions between the hotel and the guest.

The front desk agent should determine the guest's reservation status before beginning the registration process. Guests with reservation may have already undergone pre-registration activities. Guests without reservations, termed walk-in guests, present an opportunity for front desk agents to sell guest rooms. To sell successfully, the front desk agent must be very familiar with the hotel's room types, rates, and guest services and be able to describe them in a positive manner. A guest is not likely to register if he or she is not convinced of the value of renting particular room.

A registration record completed either as a part of registration activity or at the time of check in, is essential to efficient front office operation. A registration record should include information about the guests intended method of payment, the planned length of stay, and any special guest needs such as a rollaway bed, crib or a preferred guest location. It should also include the guest's billing address, telephone number and signature.

Gathering all requisite information at the time of registration enhances the front office's ability to satisfy special guest needs, forecast room occupancies, and settle guest accounts properly. At check out the guest registration card is the primary source for guest history records. The front desk agent uses the registration information to assign a room type and a room rate for each guest. It also depends on reservation information. The housekeeping should update the room status as soon as the rooms are ready for sale for efficient operation.

When assigning the guest rooms the front office assistant must also be aware of all the guest room characteristics for each room type. Hotel room types may very from standard room to the luxury suite. Furnishings, amenities and location within the property will tend to differentiate rooms within the same room type.

Once the guest decides to rent a room the front desk agents turns his or her attention to identifying the method of payment. Registration is complete once the method of payment and the guest's departure date has been established. The guest room key may be issued. When the guest arrives at the room, the occupancy stage of the guest cycle begins.

OCCUPANCY: As the center of the hotel activity, the front desk is responsible for coordinating guest services; among many services the front desk provides the guest with information. They should respond to guest's request in time and accurate to ensure guest satisfaction. A concierge my also be provided to provide special guest services.

Sound guest relations are essential for repeat visits. The front desk agents should carefully attend to guests concerns and try to seek a satisfactory resolution as quickly as possible. Security is another primary concern. Procedures for hotel and guest key control, property surveillance, safe deposit boxes, guest's personal property, and emergencies are also important. Another important job is to maintain guest folio. It has to be ensured tat house limit is taken care.

DEPARTURE: The final element of guest service is processing the check out and creating a guest history record. The final element of guest accounting is settlement of guest's account. During the checkout the front office staff should determine whether the guest was satisfied wit they stay and encourage the guest to return to the same hotel and or of same chain. The purpose of account settlement is to collect money due to the hotel prior to guest departure. Depending o n the guest's credit arrangements, guests will pay. Account balances should be verified and errors corrected before the guest leaves the hotel. Once the guest has checked out the front office analyze data related to guest's stay. Front office reports can be use d to review operations, isolate problem area, indicate where corrective action may be needed, and highlight business trends. Daily reports typically contain information about cash, and charge sales, accounts receivables and front office statistics. Operational analysis can help managers establish a standard of performance, which can be used to evaluate front office performance.

CHAPTER SEVEN

ROOM CHANGE REQUESTS

For various reasons guests may request to change rooms and this process must be conducted professionally and with as little inconvenience to the guest as possible. First, we need to check the reason for the room change. Is there something wrong with the original allocated room or is it just not what the guest has expected?

Processing a room change request

1) Establish what is wrong with the original room. This will help to decide what room you need to move the guest to and it will help maintenance or housekeeping if there is a fault with the room.

2) Check availability to enquire what rooms are available that match the guest's request.

3) Advise the guest of the room that is available to check that it is suitable before making any changes to the PMS. Advise (where appropriate) guest of the room rate for the new room and check this acceptable. In some hotels they may even take the guest to the new room to have a look.

4) Help move the guest into their new room. Usually, a porter will assist with this, giving the guest the new key, moving their luggage and taking back the old key.

5) If the guest has already spent some time in the room before the room change you will need to advise all the service departments of this room change in case the guest has put laundry into be done, been to the bar for a drink, or charged a meal to their room.

6) In a PMS system the room change will change the status of the old room from occupied too vacant/dirty. This way housekeeping knows to clean the room again. If you have a manual system you will need to call the housekeeping department and advise them of the room change

7) Update the guest folio to reflect the new room number and (if applicable) the new room rate.

In some cases, a guest may request to move to another room type that is currently not available. You can "block" or reserve the room for the guest and advise them when the change can occur. On the day of the room change the guest can pack their bags in their old room and the hotel will move them across to the new room during the day when it becomes available. All the guest has to do is pick up the new key when they arrive back at reception.

CHAPTER EIGHT

CHECK- OUT PROCEDURE

One of the last contacts the guest has with the hotel is the check-out procedure. It is also most probably the last chance for a guest to interact face to face with a hotel staff. It is, therefore, of great importance that guests' financial transactions with a hotel are properly settled before they leave.

The quality of service that guests receive at check-out will also influence their financial impressions of a hotel. A bad meal can be resurrected by a good dessert. The same is true of a guest's stay. If they had experienced some dissatisfaction with the hotel, the check-out clerks can improve their opinion of it by being friendly, courteous and efficient.

After departure, a guest's room will be available for resale to other guests. Consequently, room status information has to be updated immediately and the front office records must also be amended.

In summary, the process of check-out (usually performed by the front office cashier) involves the settlement of guests' accounts and the updating of front office records.

The main duties of the front office at check-out include:

• Settlement of guest accounts

• Updating front office records after guest departures creating good and lasting impressions

When checking out a departing guest, front office staff should follow certain basic procedures.

Here is a list of guidelines one should follow when checking out guests:

1. Greet guests. Always greet guests with a smile and say, 'Good morning' or 'Good evening' and always try to use their names.

2. Confirm guest's details (i.e. name and room number) against the guest's account.

3. Check departure date. If the guest is leaving earlier than expected, other departments will need to be informed.

4. Check whether late check-out charges should be applied. If the guest is leaving after the 12-noon check-out time, and is not a frequent guest, add the relevant late check-out charge to the account.

5. Check for late charges. Examine current entries on a guest's account, and in particular check out any mini-bar, breakfast or telephone charges.

6. Give the guest the master and/or guest folios for checking. When the guest checked in, the receptionist will have determined whether one or two folios are too produced. All queries must be handled without fuss and in a pleasant, helpful manner, in order to give a good impression of the hotel.

7. Guest settlement of accounts.

8. Provide front office services upon guest departure such as receiving the guest's key and checking if they have used a safe deposit box which now needs to be emptied.

9. Offer the assistance of the bell staff to collect the luggage.

10. See if the guest would like to make a future reservation, or an onward reservation in another hotel within the chain.

11. Update front office records. The most important records to update are the room status list and the residents list. It is important to do this, in order that other departments can accurately know the room and guest status.

A late charge is a charge for a service for facility which is sent to the cashier too late to be added to a guest's account for settlement. For example, a laundry charge may arrive at the front office cashier after the guest has already settled the bill and possibly left the hotel. In such situations, it may be difficult for a hotel to collect payment from its guests.

In order to reduce the losses due to the late arrival of charges, the cashier should confirm whether there are outstanding charges before producing the guest's accounts. The cashier may, for example, ask the guests whether they have used the mini-bar or other services that morning, and check the bill to see whether charges for breakfast that morning or other charges have been included. However, this is relying upon the honesty of the guest, and does not reflect a particularly organized or professional hotel.

This investigation of late charges is not easy and, apart from inconveniencing the guests while checks are made, it creates extra work for the busy cashier. Many hotels accept that a certain level of loss will be experienced due to late charges, and consequently charge high prices for items such as mini-bars to compensate.

To avoid and unnecessary delay and inefficient service at check-out, a well-designed and well-functioning accounting system is needed. This will ensure that:

• Guest charges from various departments are sent to the front office as soon as possible if not immediately.

• All charges are posted to the guest account once they are received. It is for these reasons that computerized accounting systems are advantageous; they greatly speed up the transfer of charge information between departments and the front desk.

Types of Settlement

The settlement of guest accounts is a comprehensive process. Accounts to be settled at check-out can be divided into two main types:

a. Own accounts - Own accounts are those accounts which will be settled by the guest. The guest may pay the bill on their departure with currency (local or foreign), personal checks, traveler's checks, bank credit cards or charge cards.

b. Company accounts - are those accounts which are not settled directly by thc guest, but are settled by a company or a travel agent. These accounts are transferred to the accounts department after the guest has checked and signed the bill as being correct. The accounts department then sends the bill and invoice to the company or travel agent for payment.

Types of Settlement

There are two main types of settlement:

1. Cash settlements

A cash settlement is any form of settlement which can be paid into the bank of the same day as it is received. Under this classification, cash settlements can include the settlements:

• in local currency

• in foreign currency

• in traveler's checks

• in personal checks

• by bank credit cards – these are cards which are issued by banks, and are considered as being equivalent to cash settlements because their imprints can be taken to the back each day, and the charge amount will be paid into a hotel's account on the same day. The best-known examples are Visa and MasterCard.

2. Credit settlements Credit settlements are settlements for which a hotel does not receive immediate payment on the day of departure. These

include:

- settlement by charge card
- settlements of corporate accounts
- travel agent vouchers

Charge cards are credit cards which are issued by private credit card organizations, e.g. American Express .

When a guest settles their account with a charge card, the hotel does not receive payment of the same day. Instead, at the end of each shift the cashier will transfer all of the bills settled by charge card to the accounts department for them to follow up at the end of the week or month, the accounts department will send out statements of the total amount charged to the private credit card organizations, together with copies of all the imprints. On receiving the statement and imprints, the credit card company will pay the amount to the hotel less its commission.

In the cases of corporate accounts and travel agent vouchers, the bills will also be transferred to the accounts department. The accounts department will then mail the account and invoice to the company or agent, and later receive a check in settlement.

Once again the travel agency will send its settlement less their commission.

Procedures for accepting settlements

The guest usually agrees the method of bill settlement upon arrival. The actual settlement process then consists of checking that the account is accurate and that the correct accounting procedures are followed

Corporate and travel agent's accounts

Very often a company or travel agent will settle only the guest-room and possibly the breakfast charges. Incidental charges such as telephone, laundry and drinks must be settled by guests themselves. In these cases, the guest account is divided into two, i.e. master accounts, settled by companies or travel agents, and incidental accounts, settled by the guests.

The different techniques for handling corporate and travel agent accounts are explained below.

	Corporate Account	Travel Agent's Account
Master	Settled by company. Shown to the guest for inspection, verification and signature at check out.	A voucher is issued by the travel agent to the guests. At check-in the voucher is collected from the guest by the receptionist. The cashier ensures that the travel agent is on the approved travel agent list (compiled by the sales and accounts department). At check-out the cashier must ensure that the guest pays for all items not covered by the voucher. The master account is not given to the guest at check-out (because the room rate paid by guest to the travel agent might not be the same as that paid by the travel agent to the hotel). After check-out the master and attached voucher will be transferred to the accounts department. At the end of the week or month the vouchers and a statement of the total account will be sent to the travel agent. Guests will be given their incidentals account for settlement.
Incidental	Settled by the guest, by cash, credit card, or personal check. A receipt is given to the guest	Settlement is usually by cash, credit card or personal check. A receipt is given to the guest.

Enter Caption

Guest of incidental accounts

Guest accounts are settled by the guests themselves, and they may choose to pay by credit card, cash, traveler's check or personal check. The procedures of accepting these forms of settlement are as follows.

On arrival when a guest proposes to settle their account by credit card, the cashier must carry out various checks. The cashier should check that:

• the card is accepted by the hotel

• the name and signature on the card are the same as those on the registration card

• the card has not passed its expiry date

• the card number is not listed on the cancellation bulletin as stolen or invalid

An imprint of the card will then be taken by the receptionist. If the guest is a walk-in or has a non-guaranteed reservation, the receptionist will pass the card through the electronic credit card machine or manually phone the credit card company for authorization.

The registration card and imprinted voucher are then handed to the cashier after check-in and stored in the bill tray. Upon check-out, when the account is finally settled by credit card, the cashier enters the bill total and date on the credit card voucher. The guest then signs the completed, detailed imprinted voucher and hands it back to the cashier, who will check to ensure that the signature matches the signature on the credit card.

During the signing of the voucher the receptionist should make the signature on the card from the guest. Should the bill be higher than the hotel's 'floor limit', then, regardless of the guest's reservation status, authorization must be obtained. A floor limit is the limit given to an establishment by the credit card company up to which a guest's bill may reach, before the hotel has to phone for permission to exceed that limit.

The last action of the cashier is to complete the guest's account. The top copy of the account, and the cardholder's copy of the credit card imprint, is given to the guest.

Accepting cash settlements

The procedures for accepting cash settlements are summarized in the table below. Bear in mind that there will be some variations in these procedures among hotels.

Method of payment	Procedures
Local currency	The cashier accepts and counts cash in front of the guest. Any change and receipt are given to the guest.
Personal checks	Do not accept a check without a check card. Is the check card limit sufficient to cover the bill? Has the check card expired? Is the signature on the card the same as on the check? Is the date correct? Does the amount in words agree with the amount in figures? Is the name of the hotel spelt correctly? Checks drawn on foreign banks and third party check should not be accepted
Traveler's checks	The cashier must ensure that the second signature on the check is written in front of them (the first signature was made when the guest collected the traveler's checks from the bank/travel agent). The cashier may also ask to see the guest's passport as a double check of identity, and record the number on the back of the checks. If the traveler's check is in a foreign currency, the cashier must calculate the foreign exchange rate conversion. All change must be given in the local currency.
Foreign	The cashier converts the bill charge into the foreign currency before account is settled. A record of the currency (foreign exchange voucher) transaction is given to the guest; this is to show the guest the exchange rate to prevent fraud. The cashier may request the guest to sign for each currency transaction as proof of acceptance. All change must be given in the local currency.

Enter Caption

Express Check- out

In most hotels guests tend to check out at approximately the same time, and consequently the cashier's desk becomes very busy during that period. Hotels therefore offer an express check-out service which allows guests to check out without having to queue at the cashier's desk. This also helps the cashier by reducing the pressure of work at busy times. In hotels with express check-out services, special forms are placed in guest-rooms as well as being available from the front office. By signing the express check-out form, the guest agrees to have the account finalized by the front office cashier after they have left the hotel.

On the morning of the date of departure, a copy of the guest's account, indicating the approximate total, may be sent to the guest's room. The guest may now leave the hotel at the convenience without having to call at the cashier's desk.

After the guest has left, the cashier will finalize the account, including any late charges, and complete the imprinted credit card voucher.

The signature on the express check-out form will replace the signature on the credit card voucher as the guest's agreement to the payment. The imprint and the signed check-out form will be sent to the credit card company for settlement. In some hotels a copy of the guest's final account is mailed to the home address of the guest so that they may check the balance on the monthly statement from the credit card company.

CREATING A GOOD LAST IMPRESSION

It is equally important that at check-out a guest should be given a good last impression. Staff who are not warm, friendly or willing to help can make guests feel unwanted and uncared for, and as a consequence they may feel that they do not want to return to the hotel. The following guidelines may help you to create a good last impression at check-out.

• The accounts must be accurate and neatly produced. Incorrect amounts mean delays to guests at the check-out des, which guest annoyance and make the front office desk, appear inefficient.

• The front office cashiers should be well trained in social skills and check-out procedures. They should be pleasant and helpful, and skilled and efficient in checking out guests. Their manner should not be so hurried that they make departing guests feel that the hotel is no longer interested in them, but should be speedily efficient.

• Sometimes, guests may have queries or complaints concerning their accounts.

These should be handled without fuss, always trying to ensure that the guest is satisfied. If a guest wishes to make a complaint, the cashier must listen patiently and with empathy. Should a guest complain and demand a reduction of the account, the cashier should again listen empathetically and do what they can to rectify the situation. However, on occasion it may become necessary to refer the matter to the front office manager.

UPDATING FRONT OFFICE RECORDS

When a guest has checked out, the front office is responsible for updating all records as soon as possible.

Room status and front office records

After a guest has checked out, their room will become vacant and will be available to other guests.

Consequently, the guest is no longer a resident of the hotel, and therefore, the room status information and front office records (e.g. the resident guest list) must be changed immediately to keep them current.

In large hotels, the updating process is automatically done by the computer. After the guest has been recorded as having checked out, the system will automatically change the room status from occupied to vacant/dirty.

The name of the guest will be removed from the residents list and transferred to the checked-out guests list and the guest's account will be transferred into a past guests file in the computer. However, it is legally required to store the registration card for 18 months.

Guest history records

In some hotels a guest history record is kept. This is a record of the guest's room and rate charged, their like and dislikes if known, as well as the amount which they spent in the hotel.

One member of the front office staff will be given the duty of the daily updating of the guest history record. The records may be kept on the computer or on handwritten cards.

When creating and updating the guest history record, a hotel will need to decide which guests should be added to the guest history records (i.e. all guests, or frequent guests only). In hotels with a computerized front office system, the computer will automatically open a new guest history record for guests who stayed in the hotel for the first time.

Stays Extensions

No matter how often you have confirmed the departure date with a guest there is still occasions when they have to stay longer than anticipated. If a guest extends their stay you will need to let housekeeping knows so they can change their cleaning schedule.

Extended Stays

Where an extension is sought, room availability needs to be checked and, if accommodation is available, then the extension can be granted. It must be remembered that an extension cannot simply be approved just because the guest is already in-house.

As a standard rule, an expected check-in/reservation takes precedence over an existing guest however you always need to take into account all relevant other factors which may include:

• If the expected check-in has confirmed or is late

• The status of the current guest and the status of the expected guest.

Preferential treatment may be given to regular guests

• Room rate being charged. A property may elect to extend a guest paying full rack rate and bump a guest who is paying a much lower room rate.

In addition, payment details need to be checked. If a guest is paying by cash, they may need to pay more cash for their extra accommodation. The fact that they have paid cash for one night may not entitle them to stay another night on credit.

Re-rooming guests

It is preferable for extending guests to stay in the same room, but this is not always possible; there may be an existing reservation that has made a special request for that room. Where the guest has to be re-roomed it is standard practice to offer porters to assist with this. Internal records also need to be adjusted to reflect the change in room number for the guest, a new key/card will have to be issued and communication sent to various departments to advise them of the change so that purchases being charged back to the room can be accurately monitored and posted.

CHAPTER TEN

Different Room Tariffs

The term tariff basically means 'rate/charge' and when it is applied to hotels, it means room rate. There are different types of room tariffs e.g. corporate rates, government rates, group rates etc. If a hotel room is not sold on a particular day that revenue is lost forever. Therefore different room tariffs have to be set. Room tariffs are decided by the management of the hotel.

The following are the various types of room rates:

a) Corporate Rate: This rate is offered to companies who send their executives for meeting to other cities. Usually a discount of 10-20% on the standard room rate is offered as part of corporate rate.

b) Crib/Child Rate: This rate is offered to families who have a child below 12 years of age with them. An extra bed called 'crib' is provided for this purpose.

c) Group Rate: This rate is offered by the hotel to those travel agents who make a group reservation at the hotel. A group usually has a minimum of 15 people.

d) Tour/Travel Agent Rate: This rate is offered by the hotel to travel agents who make individual reservations at the hotel. Usually travel agents get discounts from hotels because they give bulk business to hotels in the form of many reservations.

e) Seasonal Rate: This rate is offered by hotels when they have high business during the peak tourist season.

f) Off Season Rate: It is meant to attract guests during the low season.

g) Government Rate: This rate is offered to government officials who travel for official work.

h) Airline Rate: This rate if offered to the staff of different airlines as they have to stay in different cities/countries during their duty.

i) Complimentary Rate: This rate is offered to V.V.I.P.'S or other people who might be important for a hotel's image. Basically, it is meant for providing rooms for free.

j) Rack Rate: It is the maximum rate at which a room can be sold. Basically, the rates which are advertised by the hotels on their website and cards are the Rack rates.

CHAPTER ELEVEN

ATTRIBUTES OF FRONT OFFICE STAFF

1. Smiling Face: Smile is the most enduring competency required by front office personnel. As simple as it may seem, it is the most effective way of dealing with guests. A smile gets a smile in response. It immediately breaks down several barriers of a guest including fatigue, low spirits, doubt, anxiety etc. Always try to maintain a smile while talking to a guest. Smiling while speaking on the telephone, is a powerful way to convey tone and intention to customer who judges the caller by the voice.

2. Sense of grooming and hygiene: How you look and the first impression you create on others matters a lot. The front office personnel are the first point of physical contact for a guest with the hotel. Well groomed front office staff represents qualities of hygiene, professionalism, management style, reliability etc.

3. Punctuality: It is a hallmark of good front office staff. The front desk employee should be punctual in reporting for their shifts, as well as in the discharge of their duties and responsibilities. The punctuality of employees reflects their commitment to their work.

4. Courtesy: The hospitality industry has grown by leaps and bounds in the past decade. Whoever the guest one faces; one must be calm, patient and not be arrogant at all. This is supposed to be the basic quality that should be imbibed in all the staff of the hospitality industry. He/she should be courteous on all occasions and at all times not only towards guests but also towards colleagues and other people. The advantage and necessity of being courteous should be emphasized as it not only help operations but also ensures better relationship.

Courtesy is generally revealed by:

a) Using magic words like Thank you, Sorry, Please, "May I assist you?" I beg your pardon, Pleasure and many more. Using these words puts a great impact on the guest and makes him to feel special for an organisation.

b) Greeting the guest as per the time of the day.

c) Addressing the guest by his name as this gives him/her recognition and guest gets the feeling of personalised service

5. Voice Clarity: Voice shows the reputation or personality of the person as well as of the hotel. Cultivate voice with a smile. Tone of the voice should be cheerful, natural and unhurried, should be able to vary the pitch from time to time to lean to put warmth in voice by responsive, enthusiastic, helpful, interested and attentive.

6. Physical fitness: There are no fixed working hours in this field. One must be ready to work for round the clock and even on night shifts. Physical fitness is the utmost requirement for all the staff of hotel industry especially for front-office department because they need to stand for long hours. If an employee is physically fit it translates into energy, enthusiasm, lightness, ability to cope, youth and joy and able to serve the guest with smile and pleasure.

7. Guest oriented: Front office staff needs to be sensitive to guest's needs and demands. They should respond to them in a timely manner. Staff must put the customer as their main focus and put all thoughts and actions towards creating positive customer experience. If, the staff is not customer oriented the business of the hotel is likely to decline.

8. Disciplined: Disciplined staff provides a great support to the smooth operations of the department as well as of the hotel. Disciplined personnel properly follows house rules and regulations, tries to bring reputation and recognition to the property with his disciplined behaviour.

9. Honesty and Responsibility: There are many temptations in a hotel and provides many opportunities to front office personnel for theft of hotel and guest belongings such as money, hotel belongings (stationery items, artifacts, linen items etc. It is the moral responsibility of the employee to be loyal towards the guest and the organisation. They are responsible for not provide hotel's confidential information to other people or competitive hotels.

10.Basic etiquette: Immense work pressure, long hours of work and maintaining harmony with the clients forms an essential part of the department. All front line personnel are required to have the ability to communicate or act effectively with certain etiquette and manners.

Basic etiquettes front office personnel should exhibit includes:

a) Greet to the guest with a smiling face as per the day

b) Attend to guests as soon as they approach and if busy acknowledge his presence and assure him to be attended shortly

c) If front office staff know the guest in that case address the guest with his surname (Mr. /Ms. Kapoor). It provides the feeling of personalised service to the guest.

d) Talk politely to guest and use magic words while conversing with him/her

e) Avoid playing with pen, hair or any other item

f) Do not scratch oneself or picking the nose or ear etc.

g) Do not move hands too much while talking to guest

h) Stand erect

i) Listen guest carefully and then assist him accordingly

j) Avoid getting indulge into arguments with a guest

11.Ability to work in a team: Teamwork is one of the essential competencies. Results are the responsibility of the entire team and not the team leader alone. Team dynamics have changed over the years. A poor team performance can severely damaged the reputation of the establishment while good team performance directly enhances it

12. Good technical knowledge: Professionals can call themselves as such only when they show some physical proof of their knowledge. Employees with their knowledge and skills form the backbone of successful business. Organisations expect the true professional to convert ideas into business opportunities for the hotel. Good technical knowledge and skills makes the guest satisfied and allows hotel to get repeat guests.

Front office department of a hotel, being the first and last point of interaction for every guest has certain additional responsibility. Apart from their specific set of knowledge and skills related to their core job, they are also required to possess a certain set of behavioral skills that complete their professional profile. These behavioral skills include smile, etiquette, team work, listening, patience, grooming & personal hygiene, physical fitness etc. which will be discussed in this unit one by one.

Smile

In this competitive era a guest who is coming for stay to a particular hotel, though he is having lot of other options available because of the following reasons:

- Want to get maximum Satisfaction from the money which he is spending for his stay.
- Want to be treated in a good Manner.
- Want to give a feel that how much Important he is for the hotel.
- Want to be Listened properly for any requirement or for any complaint.
- Want to get something Extra from others.

The front office being the first interaction point can provide him all these things with a SMILE.

Meaning thereby, if a front office personal treats the guest with a SMILE the guest will feel Satisfied, he will feel that he is treated in a good Manner and how much Important his business is for the hotel, he is Listened to properly and get something Extra from others. Therefore, SMILE is an important attribute for the front office personal.

We don't realize this but a smile does make us look far more pleasant than when we do not. Besides, it does not cost us anything! The service industry considers this competency perhaps the most important one, throughout all levels of hierarchy. A smile is thus the most enduring competency required of a front office professional. As simple as it may seem, it is the most effective way of dealing with guests. A smile almost always gets a smile back in response. It immediately breaks down several barriers of the guest including fatigue, low spirits, doubt, anxiety and dissatisfaction. Recruitment personnel see it as the first sign of front office professionalism at the time of interview. It is recommended that professionals smile in front of the mirror and assess their competency in it. It is recommended to smile while speaking on the telephone because it is a powerful way to convey tone and intention to the customer who judges the caller by his/her voice.

Etiquette

The first interaction of a guest in the hotel is with front office personal, and on the basis of this interaction he makes an image of the hotel in his mind, now this image may be good or bad and this depends upon how the front office person has interacted and behaved with the guest. To make a positive image in the mind of the guest the front office personal must behave with the guest in good manner and this behaving in good manner is called as Etiquette. The Etiquette may be defined as code of behavior among people within an organization, group or society. The basic etiquettes that a front office staff should exhibit with the guests are as follows.

1. Welcome the guest, wishing a customer the time of the day and saying _Thank You' is the basic etiquettes that must be shown by the front office personal

2. Smile and attend to guests as soon as they approach the front desk. If busy, acknowledge their presence in words assuring them that they will be attended to shortly.

3. Talk softly and politely.

4. Recognize guests, recognition is a powerful tool that plays a great role in retaining regular guests. The use of their name gives them importance and a feeling of belonging.

5. Stand erect at all the times.

6. The special needs of the guest like choice of room like smoking room or non smoking room must be taken due attention.

7. Help the guest in filling the registration form or by providing them information as requested by them.

8. Don't argue with the guest also don't argue with your colleagues in front of the other guests.

9. Anticipate the guest needs for example hand him a pen, light his cigarette, reach out for the bag he is carrying.

10. Do not get familiar with the guest even if he treats you like a friend remember your relationship with the guest is professional.

11. Be aware about offensive habits you have like biting nails, picking hair, nose, ear, yawning, Sneezing/couching without covering your mouth. Refrain at least, when you are in guest's view.

12. Do not speak poorly about other guests, staff or departments.

13. Speak softly and politely and do not use much of slang and frequently use the terms such as _thank you', _May I help you', _Excuse me', _Pardon me' etc.

14. Carry pencils in the trouser pockets and not behind ears or clipped in front of the jacket.

15. Do not chew gum.

16. Present the bill to the host discretely so as to avoid embarrassing him/her and give sufficient time to check him his or her bill.

17. Use service doors only for entering and exit at the front office.

18. If you are on phone beware of your conversion on the telephone guest may be watching or hearing you so avoid things like shouting on the telephone, long conversation, personal calls at work etc.

19. Never shouts on the telephone

Team Work

Another attribute which a front office personal must have is team work. Without proper teamwork nothing can be done successfully in this world especially in the service industry. Teams play a very prominent role in hospitality industry. A poor team performance surely damages the reputation of an establishment, while a superior team performance directly increases its reputation. Teamwork can be seen only once the person has been recruited, though it is an essential attribute. Team dynamics have changed over the years. Let us discuss the dynamics of teamwork .

Team: A Team comprises a group of people linked in common purpose, a team is a small inter-dependent group of people with complementary skills who work committed towards a common purpose, performance goals and approach for which they hold themselves mutually accountable. The key works are interdependence (depending on each other), complementary skills (essential yet different skills that are needed to complete a given task well) and accountability (ownership of results). No one person can deliver any goals on his own. It takes a team to deliver results with complementary specializations with the desire to accomplish objectives and hold themselves responsible for a success or failure.

Need for Team: Teams can meet significant performance challenges together. They have a common purpose and move together towards it. Team members understand each other's strengths and drawbacks well and are able to assist or motivate a weaker team member. They harness complementary skills of other team members and trust their own competency at the same time. They can be a positive influence on each other with regard to be ethics and discipline.

Team in Front Office Operation: Being the centre department of the hotel, front office needs to coordinate with almost each and every department of the hotel but still in the direct teams of front office operation are the telecommunications, the people working at guest relation desk, lobby staff, cashier. Each has distinct skills to make a guest's stay comfortable. The indirect teams in the front office operations are purchase, stores, IT, food and beverages, and engineering who work towards making the operations system strong enough to deliver good service. The respond to guest needs expressed to the front office as also keep the front desk functional.

Team Leader's Role: The team leader's role is to build commitment to the common purpose by example. He uses leadership as a means to an end and not as a weapon to show superiority. The leaders fills in gaps in competencies, delegates work, is hands-on performers with the team, makes key decisions, manage external relationships including the management, guests, and the government and lends support in a crisis.

Team Member's Quality: Team members are performers who take joy in working together. They take responsibility for the job and understand its objectives in a larger perspective. They hold themselves accountable together, for success or failure. They have a sense of urgency with youthful enthusiasm and energy. They are result-oriented and respect each other. Below are few of the qualities of team members.

Attitude: An attitude can be defined as an outlook towards life. In other words, attitude is something that we own and are responsible for. It comes from within and can be positive or negative, based on one's experiences as well as the environment in which one lives. Few of the attitudes of front office personal are as follows:

1. In hospitality industry people give business to those who give better service so the front office personal must feel joy in serving the people. A good service not only gets better pay cheques and tips but also promotes customer loyalty.

2. Every single employee must have an attitude of ownership of the hotel. Only then he will show commitment, maintain the quality of service and take pride in the hotels appearance.

3. Co-operation is vital in team performances. It brings about positivity in work.

4. Initiative is a valuable competency in today's world. The only way to beat competition is to innovate and bring in new ideas. The front office personal must always look for new ideas and introduce them.

5. Honesty is a precious attribute. There are opportunities for theft of property and guest belongings, misleading guests with information, giving secrets to competition etc. Organizations value and reward employees who have shown uprightness and honesty in situations where they could have been otherwise.

Listening

"We were given two ears but only one mouth, because listening is twice as hard as talking." Especially for front office personal, as the guests hates having to repeat a request or instruction. While the guest is talking about his problem or giving any information the front office person must use the LISTEN meaning thereby is.

L — Look

I — Inquire

S — Summarize

T — Take Notes

E — Encourage

N — Neutralize

Look: look at the guest you are speaking to, with a good eye contact and the eyes must stand quiet.

Inquire: ask good questions to clarify like what, which, who, why, when, how etc. all this reflects that you are interested in listening to the guest and ask him to tell you more.

Summarize: frequently summarize your understanding about what the guest is saying, use the worlds like —Let me just summarize my understanding‖.

Take Note: take notes of important point on a piece of paper because human memory is limited and can not remember all the things.

Encourage: stay calm and smile, and encourage the guest to say more.

Neutralize: neutralize your feeling, what you think on this complaint or on suggestion avoid biasness at this stage.

Front office personal must show the effective listening skills to make the guest satisfied. Don‘t avoid the guest just because he is having a slow or monotonous voice or he is not very good in expressing himself.

Patience

Patience is another attribute which is required in front office personal. Sometimes because of the systems and procedures of the hotel the guest become frustrated and start shouting on the front office executive or because of certain break down his work get hampered and he is annoyed. Front office must handle these situations with patience; means he need to remain cool and calm. The following things can be taken care off if these kind of situations arise:

Listen: Listen the guest carefully it is important for the front office staff to divorce himself from the emotions expressed and understand the nature of the problem thoroughly

Apologize: Apologize to the guest. An apology is the least that a guest expects Give directions: Give directions if it seems a problem that can be handled by the guest. For example the guest may complain that the television not working.

It could be simple thing that the main electrical socket is switched off or the cord to the television is not connected. These directions must be given politely but clearly.

Exact Action: Tell the guest the exact action that will be taken. For example the front office personal can say —I inform the maintenance immediately, who will be in touch with you shortly.

Follow-up: Follow up with the servicing department and the guest if action has been taken Even if action is not taken, guests like to know that someone is following up the matter.

The front office personal should not lose temper, which can create a big problem.

If the executive at the front office is unable to handle the customer immediately, he must call his supervisor to handle the guest.

Personal Hygiene and Grooming

In personal hygiene & grooming we will discuss the following things which the front office personal must take care of.

- Hair
- Nails
- Ornaments
- Footwear
- Make Up
- Uniform

Hair: Well kept hairs are indicator of proper grooming. It makes front desk personnel presentable to the guest and enhances the first impression of the hotel in view of guest.

Grooming standards for Hair for male

- The hairs should not fall on the forehead and should not touch either ear or collars.
- Must be neatly combed and should not be oily.
- Conservative and well maintained hair style must be used.
- The hair should be clean, odder free and must be free from dandruff.
- The hair should not extend more than the nape of the neck
- The hair should be trimmed above the color.
- Moustaches should e neatly trimmed and should not cover upper lips.
- The face must be clean shaved.

- The sideburns must be well trimmed and cut straight at the tip and should not exceed half the length of ear.
- Beards are only permitted for religious reasons and must be suitable maintained.

Grooming Standards for hair for female

- The hairs should be trimmed regularly and must be styled away from the face.
- Black accessories like black pin can be used if required to keep hair neat and in place.
- French knot can be used to keep the hair away from the face.
- The colored or plastic bands should not be used.
- Ponytail can be made but should not be longer than 9"
- Like man the hair should be clean, odder free and must be free from dandruff.

Nails

- In case of both male and female the nails should be well maintained neatly cut, clean and must be dirt free
- There should not be any stains of nicotine or carbon or any ink stains.
- Incase of female the nails should not be excessively long.
- Only prescribed nail polish should be used which must cover the entire nail with no gaps or cracks.
- In case of female the toe nail polish should match the finger nail polish

Ornaments

- For male, only one single ring on any of the one hand can be used and for female one ring on each hand can be used but that must be of conservative and sober.
- The males should not use any bracelets or bands in any of the hands only for religious reasons the bracelets can be used while female can use two thin bangles either of gold or silver in any of the hand or one in each hand.
- The females can also wear one thing gold chain either of gold or silver and they can also wear a small nose stud.

- The watches if used should be of conservative in style should not be too large and flashy.
- If leather strap is used it must be in black or in brown color and if metallic strap is used it must be either in gold or in silver color.
- The females can wear one set of earrings but those should not be flashy or too large.

Footwear

- Males must wear black or brown shoes which should be of oxford styles and must be polished and in good repair, females must wear closed shoes or sandals which should be polished and must be in good repair.
- Females shoes should not be flat and minimum heel should be ½ "
- The socks should be clear and odorless, should not have any patterns and there elastic must be intac

Makeup

Makeup is used by female personal in the hotel and they should take care of the following things.

- The foundation must be used to avoid the oily look.
- The color of lipstick should be of matte finish, sober, and must match with the uniform and matching lip liner must be used.
- For eye shadow darker shade over the eyelids and lighter shades below the eyebrow can be used.
- Start by applying the mascara to the upper eyelashes brush downward and then upward.
- The bindis should be small, round or tear shaped and single shade of sober color the matches the uniform must be used.

Uniform: Uniform plays many role like identification of department of hotel employee, protective covering for employee and many more. It enhance confidence in the employee.

Uniform male

- The uniform must be immaculate, spotless well ironed and should not have unnecessary creases.

- The uniform should be of perfect fit, should not be faded and must appear fresh
- There should not be loose threads or broken buttons.
- The cuffs and collars must be clean and stain free.
- A simple belt can be weared but the buckle should not be too flashy and should not be wide more than 1.5 "
- The name tag should be shining and must be visible

Uniform female

The sarees are being weared by the female personal in the hotel and the following things should be considered while wearing a saree.

- The saree should be pinned neatly and the pins should not be visible
- The saree must be immaculate, smooth, clean no creases or stains.
- The high neck blouse must be weared and the sleeves of the blouse must be till elbows.
- The name tag should be shining and must be prominently displayed.

Pleasant Personality

Most often, a front desk employee is the first person with whom a guest comes in contact. The guest starts building the image of the hotel from the physical appearance and personality of the front office personal. The gestures, grooming, and personal presentation of a front desk employee are very important in leaving a good impression in the mind of the guest. The front desk personnel should be well turned out; they should have a pleasant personality, greeting guests with a smiling face and showing interest in their concerns.

CHAPTER TWELVE

YIELD MANAGEMENT

Yield management in the hotel industry is a dynamic pricing strategy for maximizing revenue from a fixed, time-limited inventory, such as hotel rooms.

It's based on understanding and predicting consumer behavior to influence future hotel guests and generate maximum revenue per available room (RevPAR).

In simpler terms, yield management in hotels refers to selling the right room to the right customer at the right time and at the right price or rate.

Concept of yield management

Airlines were the first industry where the yield management concept used. In face any industry which deals in perishable product the yield management concept is very useful. Like airlines, this concept is more popular in hotels, restaurants, car rental, bus rental, cruises, railways etc. Yield management is based on supply and demand formula. As and when the demand increases the supply the price increases and on the contrary if demand is less than the supply then the price decreases. During off season low price booking is accepted but during peak season only high price booking are taken. In peak season even up selling is recommended.

The demand forecast assists front office manager whether the price should be lowered or increased, and whether a reservation request should be accepted or refused in order to maximize the revenue. Hotel's manager biggest problem is that neither they can increases the supply of rooms in case of more demand nor they can store it and sell on the following days in case of rooms left unsold on a particular day.

Yield management control forecast information in three ways to maximize revenue and these are:

Capacity management

Discount allocation

Duration control

Capacity Management: Cancellation at last moment and no-shows can never be eliminated. Capacity management means over booking. With experience front office decides that how much over booking should be done so that cent percent or more than cent percent booking may be achieved. In case of over booking, it is always safe to request the similar hotels near by to hold few rooms in case of emergency and overflow of guests holding guaranteed/confirmed booking can be diverted to the other hotels and hotel can pay for their cab fare and even difference in room tariff. Capacity management also include determining how many walk-ins should be accepted on the day of arrival based on expected cancellations, no-shows, late arrival and early morning departure.

Discount Allocation: Discounting means selling rooms at a price lower then rack rates. Room is a perishable product. It is better to sell it at discount then to keep it vacant. Moreover a room sale will also increase the food sale. If possible hotel can offer high value rooms at the single or double room rack rate instead of giving discount on single or double room.

Duration Control: In case on certain date say 10th October only a few rooms are available but on the dates before say 7th, 8th, 9th and after that date say 11th, 12th, 13th rooms are available then hotel may refuse a booking request for 10th October only. Hotel will prefer to sell rooms for 10th October if there is a demand for some other days as well either before 10th or after 10th October. This will help hotel in optimizing room revenue. But if all the dated from 7th October to 12th October most of the rooms are sold and there is a reservation request for 10th October only then hotel may accept it as other dates are already booked.

METHODS ADOPTED FOR EVALUATING PERFORMANCE OF OPERATIONS

- Occupancy %
- ARR

DISADVANTAGES OF OCCUPANCY % AND ARR AS PERFORMANCE MEASURE

- One Dimensional Approach Relationship between the two is neglected.
For eg; Lower Room Rate = Higher Occupancy
Higher Room Rate = Lower Occupancy
But ARR does not increase
- Cost per Occupied Room is neglected

REVENUE MANAGEMENT/ YIELD MANAGEMENT

[Combines the two factors Occupancy% and ADR into one statistic]

Revenue management is an evaluative tool that allows the front office manager to use the potential revenue as a standard against which actual revenue can be compared.

WHAT IS YIELD

Yield is

➢ The final product after processing

➢ Revenue generated per statistical unit

➢ Yield = Output = revenue

➢ Therefore, yield management = revenue management

➢ Yield is the total output and depends upon facts

ORIGIN

➢ Concept introduced by the airline industry in 1970's

➢ Sold perishable seats at rack rates

➢ Adopted a technique based on Demand & Supply

➢ Demand exceeded supply = increase the rate and supply exceeds demand = demand the rate

➢ Demand exceeded supply = increase the rate and supply exceeds demand = demand the rate

➢ Yield management was referred as revenue per available seat per mile.

APPLICATION OF YIELD MANAGEMENT/ REVENUE MANAGEMENT

Applied in segments with perishable product

• Airlines Revenue per available seat

• Car rental per car Revenue per available seat

• Restaurant per hr Revenue per available seat

• Hotel per night Revenue per available room

CONDITIONS FOR THE APPLICATION OF YIELD MANAGEMENT

1. Fixed amount of resources for sale

- Airline seats, hotel rooms

2. Resources sold are perishable

- Tomorrow, hotels sells tomorrows room

3. Differential pricing

- Customers willing to pay different price for using the same resources.

Thus, yield management is

➢ Understanding

➢ Anticipating

➢ Influencing

Consumer behaviour in order to maximise revenue/ profits from a fixed perishable resource.

"Technique based on demand and supply used to maximize revenues by lowering prices to increase sales during periods of low demand and raising prices during periods of high demands."

CHALLENGE IS:

- The right INVENTORY to
- The right CUSTOMER at
- The right TIME at
- The right PRICE

COMPONENTS OF YIELD MANAGEMENT

- Fixed inventory
- Potential customer
- Differential pricing
- Time: Peak seasons and off seasons
- Channel: Travel portals, CRS

POINTS TO BE CONSIDERED

Predict consumer behaviour

➢ Length of stay

➢ Buying capacity

Optimize the prize and inventory available to each customer segment

➢ Discounts

➢ Packages

➢ Apply rack rates

Focus on revenue maximization than on cost minimization

➢ Do not cut on facilities and amenities

➢ Effect quality and brand name

Marginal cost which is involved in cleaning and supplies will be incurred only if the room is sold.

➢ Loss to hotels operating cost

GOAL OF YIELD MANAGEMENT

To select which business to accept and which business to turn away!

BUSINESS TACTICS FOR HIGH AND LOW DEMANDS

Industries use some practices to maximize the revenue.

In order to implement these tactics, management needs to establish the HURDLE RATE (the lowest rate for a given day) below which it is impossible to sell any room.

HIGH DEMAND TACTICS

- Close or restrict discounts
- Apply minimum length of stay
- Reduce group reservations
- Reduce or eliminate 6 PM holds
- Apply early deposits to maximize early departures.
- Raise room rates

➢ Executive and suite rooms

LOW DEMAND TACTICS

- Sell hotel facilities and benefits
- Offer packages
- Accept discounts to encourage room nights
- Encourage and provide incentives to staff for increasing occupancy
- Encourage upgrades
- Remove stay restrictions

➢ Encourage guest to overstay in case of low occupancy

Establish relationships with competitors to share

➢ Referrals

➢ Marketing strategies

Offer stay-sensitive price incentives

➢ Provide discounts for guest who stays longer

➢ Guest with a five days stay may get a discount while a guest with two days stay may not.

➢ Provide freebies like movie tickets, site seeing, shopping coupons from the hotel's concessionaire

IMPORTANCE OF YIELD MANAGEMENT

1. Improved forecasting
2. Improved seasonal pricing and inventory management
3. Identification of new market segments
4. Identification of new market segment demands
5. Increased coordination between front office and sales
6. Determination of discounting activity
7. Improved short term and long-term planning
8. Increased business and profits

How Do You Calculate Yield Management?

The formula for calculating yield management is as follows:

Yield Management = (Achieved Revenue / Maximum Potential Revenue) * 100

Example: If your hotel has 70 rooms that you sell for INR-300 each, your maximum potential revenue would be INR-21,000. Suppose you sell 50 rooms at INR-250 each on a particular night. Your achieved revenue for that night would be INR-12,500. That means that your yield percentage would be 59.5%.

Yield Management vs. Revenue Management

There's a fine line between yield management and revenue management.

Yield management has a narrow scope, focusing only on room prices and sales volume for generating maximum revenue from occupancy, that is, through inventory control.

Revenue management considers the selling price and sales volume, but it focuses on much more than just revenue yield from occupancy. It includes the cost of selling and all the other revenue sources within your hotel, such as food and beverage outlets, wellness centers, and other amenities.

It involves segmenting markets and forecasting demand to predict consumer behavior and optimize your services' prices and availability. As such, revenue management helps you boost your hotel's overall revenue growth.

CHAPTER THIRTEEN

Front Office Accounting

It is a systematic process in which the front office accounting staff identifies, records, measures, classifies, verifies, summarizes, interprets, organizes, and communicates financial information for a hotel business.

Basic Front Office Accounting Formula

Net Outstanding Balance = Previous Balance + Debit – Credit

Where debit increases the outstanding balance and credit decreases it. Most of the contemporary hotel businesses employ automated accounting system.

Hotel Accounting Terms

Account: A collection of all transactions incurred by a guest.

Folio: A statement of all transactions that affect the balance of an account.

Posting: The process of recording transactions onto a folio.

Types Of Accounts

Guest Account: It is the record of financial transactions between hotel and in-house guest. Such accounts are created at the time of guest guaranteed reservation or at the registration of the guest in the hotel. During the stay the front office looks for any transactions held by guests and posts the same in guest folio. The payments of the accounts is generally taken at the checkout stage of the guest, but in some cases a guest may be requested to make partial or full payment during any time of guest cycle. It may be seen when a guest crosses house limit set by the hotel for every individual guest.

Non-guest Account: In order to promote local business and corporates business, hotel might extend charge privilege to such guests, groups and for them non-guest accounts may be created. Non-guest account may be formed even for those guests who do not settle their account completely, hence changing their status from guest to non-guest. The non-guest accounts are generally billed monthly by the hotel accounting section.

Types Of Folios

Guest Folio: Front office is responsible during occupancy

Non-guest Folio: Used for house accounts

Master Folio: Used for group accounts

Incidental Folio: Used when folios are split

Account Settlements

There are various issues regarding account settlement –

Orientation of Account Settlement

By Guest – The guest settles own account by cash/credit card/cheque.

By Organization – The organization settles guest account by transferring money to the hotel account.

Methods of Account Settlement

There are following popular methods of account settlement –

Account Settlement in Local Currency – A guest can pay in terms of a local currency where the payment is not chargeable with conversion fees.

Account Settlement in Foreign Currency – If the guest prefers to pay in foreign currency, the service of payment by the bank is chargeable for around 3% to 6% of the total payable amount.

Account Settlement Using Traveler Check – Travelers' cheques, the pre-printed cheques in the denominations of major world currencies are a good option to paying by cash.

Debit Card – Use of magnetic cards for payment against account is most common today. Paying by debit cards is as good as paying by cash as the amount of money is instantly transferred from the guest's bank account into the hotel's bank account.

In case of credit card settlement, the accounting staff mails the charge vouchers signed by guests to the credit card company; preferably within a specified time. The credit card company then settles the guest account by transferring money against it.

Credit Settlement by Organization – Many national, international, private, or public organizations send their employees or students for attending workshops, seminar, or meetings. Such organizations tie-up with the hotel for paying the bills of their employees on credit. The organizations reserve accommodations depending on the number of room nights (number of rooms × number of nights the representatives are expected to occupy). This is popularly known as account Settlement using Direct Billing.

In direct billing account settlement, the front office staff verifies guest folios and transfers the guest account to non-guest or city account. The hotel's back-office accounting verifies the guest folios and is responsible to collect the direct billing amount from a direct billing agency such as embassy, university, or organizations.

The accounting section also notifies the guests that if the direct billing agency fails or refuses to pay the charges then the guests need to settle the account by paying them from their pocket.

Combined Account Settlement – A guest can settle account by paying partial amount in cash and remaining amount on credit. The front office staff needs to prepare the supporting document for such kind of payment and hands it over to the back-office accounts.

Voucher

These are documents that have details of transactions made by guests from various point of sales in hotels like, room service, restaurant, etc. The voucher is sent to front office for posting in the guest's folio and record keeping. Vouchers acts as a supporting document of the transaction happened between the hotel and the guest. A voucher also acts as a proof that a transaction has taken place in the hotel. Charge vouchers, Correction vouchers, Allowance vouchers, Transfer vouchers and Paid Out vouchers are examples of vouchers.

A voucher details a transaction to be posted to a front office account. There are several types of vouchers used in front office accounting system:

1. Cash Voucher – A voucher used to support a cash payment transaction at the front desk.

2. Charge Voucher – A voucher used to support a charge purchase transaction that takes place somewhere other than the front office.

3. Allowance Voucher – A voucher used to support an account allowance.

4. Cash Advance Voucher – A voucher used to support cash flow out of the hotel, either directly to or on behalf of the guest.

5. Correction Voucher – A voucher used to support the correction of a posting error which is rectified before the close of business on the day the error was made.

6. Credit Card Voucher – A form designated by the credit card company to be used for imprinting the credit card and recording the amount charged.

7. Paid-Out Voucher – A voucher used to support the cash disbursed by the hotel on behalf of a guest. 8. Transfer Voucher – A voucher used

to support a reduction in balance on one folio and an equal increase in balance on another. Transfer vouchers are used for transfers between guest accounts and for transfers from guest accounts to non-guest accounts when they are settled by credit cards.

9. Travel Agency Voucher – In travel agent guaranteed reservation, the travel agent forwards a voucher to the hotel as proof of payment and guarantees that the prepaid amount will be sent to the hotel when the voucher is returned to the travel agency for payment.

Daily Reports

The daily report contains key operating ratios such as room occupancy percentage (ROP), which is the number of rooms occupied divided by the number of rooms available:

rooms Occupied / rooms available

Thus, if a hotel has 850 rooms and 622 are occupied, the occupancy percentage is 622 · 850 = 73 percent. The average daily rate (ADR) is calculated by dividing the rooms revenue by the number of rooms sold:

rooms revenue / rooms Sold

If the rooms revenue is 75,884 and the number of rooms sold is 662, then the ADR is 114.63. The ADR is, together with the occupancy percentage, one of the key operating ratios that indicates the hotel's performance.

Room occupancy percentage (ROP):

If total available rooms are 850

And total rooms occupied are 622

Then:

Occupancy percentage = (622/850) × 100 = 73%

Average daily rate: If rooms revenue is 75,884

And total number of rooms sold is 622

Then: rooms Occupied rooms available Average daily rate = 75,884 / 662 = 114.63

Night Auditor

A hotel is one of the few businesses that balances its accounts at the end of each business day. Because a hotel is open 24 hours every day, it is difficult to stop transactions at any given moment. The night auditor and his or her team wait until the hotel quiets down at about 1:00 a.m., and then begins the task of balancing the guests' accounts receivable.

The process of night auditing is as follows:

1. The night audit team runs a preliminary reconciliation report that shows the total revenue generated from room and tax, banquets and

catering, food and beverage outlets, and other incidentals (phone, gift shop, etc.).

2. All errors on the report are investigated.

3. All changes are posted and balanced with the preliminary charges.

4. A comparison of charges is carried out, matching preliminary with actual charges.

5. Totals for credit card charges, rooms operations, food and beverages, and incidentals are verified.

6. The team "rolls the date"—they go forward to the next day.

7. Post any charges that the evening shift was not able to post.

8. Pass discrepancies to shift managers in the morning. The room and tax charges are then posted to each folio and a new balance shown.

9. Run backup reports so that if the computer system fails, the hotel will have up-to-date information to operate a manual system.

10. Reconcile point-of-sale and PMS to guest accounts. If this does not balance, the auditor must balance it by investigating errors or omissions. This is done by checking that every departmental charge shows up on guest folios.

11. Complete and distribute the daily report. This report details the previous day's activities and includes vital information about the performance of the hotel.

12. Determine areas of the hotel where theft could potentially occur.

Larger hotels may have more than one night auditor, but in smaller properties these duties may be combined with night manager, desk, or night watchperson duties.

Ledgers

A Ledger is a book in which the account summary of both resident and non-resident guests are entered. The front office ledger is a collection of front office account folios. They are the part of accounts receivable ledger. An account receivable ledger represents money owed to the hotel. Moreover, this ledger aids in preparing the Profit and Loss account and Balance Sheet of a hotel. Front office accounting system separates accounts receivable ledger in two groups. The guest ledger and the nonguest ledger.

Guest ledger: Guest Ledger is a type of ledger that has the accounts of all the guests staying in a hotel or guests who have sent advance deposit. All financial transactions made by a guest are recorded onto guest folio opened at the time of registration to assist tracking guest account balances. This ledger is also known as Transient or Room Ledger. Guests who make appropriate credit arrangements at registration may be extended privileges to charge purchases to their individual account folios. Guests may also pay against their outstanding balance at any time during occupancy. Guest's financial transactions are recorded in guest ledger accounts to track guest account balances. Some of the accounts of the resident guests may be settled by their company, travel agency or Airline Company.

City Ledger: The City ledger is also known as the Non-guest ledger and it is the collection of non-guest accounts. If a guest account is not settled by the guest in full at checkout, the guest's folio balance is transferred from the guest ledger to the city ledger in the accounting division for collection post departure of the guest. City Ledger could also include accounts held by local business people using hotel facilities and services for entertainment or business meetings. Guests who walk out of the hotel without settling the outstanding balance. Guests who have sent prepayments to guarantee their bookings, but have not arrived or checked in. Even a skipper's outstanding balance is transferred to city ledger with a hope that the amount may come through.

Accounting System

The formats of guest and non-guest account folios may be different, depending upon the front office recordkeeping system. The process of guest accounting is operated either:-

Manually i.e., non-automated: In this operating mode all the phases involved in accounting process are carried out by the staff. Guest folios in a manual system contain a series of columns for listing individual debit and credit entries accumulated during occupancy. At the end of the business day, each column is totalled and the ending balance is carried forward as the opening folio balance of the following day. The entire system is prone to omission and computation errors. Another drawback is handling and re-handling of numbers data. This type of system is useful for small hotels only where the workload is not much.

Mechanically i.e., semi-automated: This system is used by hotels which are medium-sized or large but yet don't have automatic machines like computers. Usually they use a combination of office machines, clerical equipment and manpower to operate these systems. Guest transactions are printed sequentially on a machine-posted folio. The information recorded for each transaction includes the date, department or reference number, amount of the transaction, and new balance of the account. The folios outstanding balance is the amount the guest owes to the hotel or the amount the hotel owes the guest in the event of credit balance at settlement. If the posting is done by mechanical equipment, it does not retain individual folio balances. This means that each accounts previous balance must be reentered each time an account posting is made to the folio.

Through Computer i.e., fully automated: This system comprises of computers and other electronic devices located at every point of sale and interfaced with the main cashier at the front desk. All task done manually is easily done by automatic machines whether it's posting, auditing, correction of errors, etc. The machines are fast and practically no possibility of late charges. Necessary steps such as sorting, of vouchers, identification, posting code and reference code, posting are automatically carried out. Since computers are machines operated by humans, it is obvious that the accuracy will depend upon the software developed and the efficiency of the staff operating.

Guest Weekly Bill

Guest weekly bill is prepared for each guest and is presented on checkout for settlement. It is called a weekly bill as for one week one bill is prepared. There is no hard and fast rule that a bill has to be prepared for one week. In case majority of guests in a hotel stay for three days then one may adopt a three day bill. If a guest stays beyond three days then another bill is attached. The guest weekly bill is opened immediately on check in by receptionist. The copy of the guest registration card is stapled with the weekly bill/folio. The cashier can refer to guest's signature on guest registration card and compare his/her signature with the voucher. If signature tallies then the cashier debits the voucher to guest's account otherwise he/she sends the bill back to the outlet with a remark that signature does not tally. All the weekly bills are placed numerically in the vertical file and it helps in taking out a particular bill instantly. The vouchers after posting in the guest weekly bill should be kept in the bills rack.

Front office Accounting cycle-Creation, Maintenance and settlement of accounts:-

FRONT OFFICE ACCOUNTING SYSTEM FORMULA Transaction postings in the front office conform to a basic accounting formula, which Previous Balance + Debits – Credits = Net Outstanding Balances

INTERNAL CONTROL IN THE FRONT OFFICE Internal control in the front office involves:

• Tracking transaction documentation

• Verifying account entries and balances

• Identifying vulnerabilities in the accounting system

Auditing is a process of verifying front office accounting records for accuracy. Certain records are maintained to have a control in front office cash:

• FRONT OFFICE CASH SHEET – The front office is responsible for a variety of cash transactions affecting both guest and non-guest accounts. The front office cashiers have to complete a front office cash sheet that lists each receipt or disbursement of cash.

• CASH BANK – A cash bank is the amount of cash assigned to a cashier so that he/she can handle the various transactions that occur during a particular work shift. Cashiers should sign for their bank at the beginning of their shift and only the person who signs should have access to it.

NET CASH RECEIPTS = Amount of Cash, Checks, Vouchers etc in the Cashier's Drawer – [Amount of Initial Cash Bank + Paid Outs]

OVERAGES – When the total of cash and checks in a cash drawer is greater than the initial cash bank + net cash receipts

SHORTAGES – When the total of cash and checks in a cash drawer is less than the initial cash bank + net cash receipts.

DUE BACK – A due back occurs when a cashier pays out more than he/she receives i.e. there is not enough cash in the cash drawer to restore the initial cash bank. This may happen when a cashier accepts many checks, or encashes large amount of foreign exchange offered by a guest during shifts. These checks and bills are deposited with other receipts and consequently the front office deposit may be greater than the cashier's net cash receipts, with the excess due back to the front office cashier's bank.

• AUDIT CONTROL – Internal auditors should make unannounced visits to the front office cashier's desk for auditing accounting records as well as conducting spot checks of the cash bank of the cashier on duty. A report should be completed for management and ownership review.

SETTLEMENT OF ACCOUNTS The collection of payment for outstanding account balances is called account settlement which involves bringing the account balance to zero. An account can be brought to zero balance as a result of a cash payment in full or a transfer to an approved direct billing or credit card account. All guest accounts must be settled at the time of check out.

Credit control measures-Pre-Authorization, Advance Payments, Floor Limit, House Limit

CREDIT MONITORING :The front office accounting system must monitor guest and non-guest accounts to ensure that they remain within acceptable credit limits.

• Guests who present an acceptable credit card at registration may be extended credit facility equal to the floor limit authorized by the issuing credit card company.

• Guest and non-guest accounts with other approved credit arrangements are subject to limitations established by the front office called house limit.

• The night auditor is mainly responsible for identifying accounts which have reached or exceeded the fixed credit limits. Such accounts are called high risk or high balance accounts. The front office may deny additional charge purchase privileges to such accounts.

• This situation may be resolved by requesting the guest to make a partial payment or requesting the credit card company to authorize additional credit.

During the stay, guest is offered various facilities and services like room, food, beverage, health club, telephone, etc. For each of these services the payment is expected either at the time of service rendered or on or after the departure time. In order to present the final bill, with all vouchers duly debited, a proper record of all the vouchers is recorded in the guests' folio and in guest ledgers. The front office ability to collect outstanding balances depends upon the usage and performance of the accounting system followed by hotels. An effective accounting system consists of performed during various stages of guest cycle. At the pre-arrival stage a guest accounting system gathers data related to reservation guarantee and any advance deposits. At the time of guest arrival, the accounting system looks for room rates assigned and the taxes/discounts applicable at the registration. During the occupancy stage the transactions of the guest are tracked and posted to the folios. Lastly, at the departure stage, guest accounting system ensures payment for facilities and services availed by the guest.

CHAPTER FOURTEEN

Revenue management

Revenue management is a strategic function in maximizing room revenue (REV PAR) along with growing market share. REV PAR and market share are the two primary barometers used in the industry to grade a revenue manager's competency. It is essential for revenue managers to have a system in place for daily business reviews to formulate winning strategies. Daily duties include:

1. Analyzing Data: A revenue manager must develop a reporting system for daily monitoring. In recent years, the larger hotel brands have developed proprietary revenue management systems that provide on-demand reporting of historical data, future position, and the ability to apply real-time pricing changes to future nights. Understanding past performance can uncover various business trends over high and low demand periods. It is critical to understand the effectiveness of previous pricing strategies to better position the hotel on future nights. The general public can view rates and book rooms up to 365 days into the future. Therefore, the revenue manager must monitor daily pickup in reservations and regrets for future nights and make necessary adjustments to enhance speed to market. Each hotel will have different booking windows (or lead times) for their transient and group business. For example, the X market has a majority of transient bookings that occur within 120 days to arrival, whereas the group business is booked many months out, and in some cases several years in advance. The primary booking window must be analyzed on a daily basis and adjusted accordingly. The longer booking windows can be analyzed periodically with the director of sales to equip the Sales team with rates to book group business based on the hotel's revenue goals.

2. Mix of Business Assessment: Finding the right balance of occupancy and ADR could yield the greatest REV PAR and is greatly influenced by the mix of business. It is composed of two primary customer segments:

Transient (individual travelers for business or leisure) and Groups, which are bookings with 10 more rooms per night (i.e., conventions, company meetings, etc.). Hotels can differ with mixes of business based on location, number of rooms, and event space. Convention hotels may have a desired mix of 80 percent group and 20 percent transient to achieve their optimum point of profit, whereas small to midsize hotels may have a need for greater transient business, all of which are key factors in formulating effective pricing strategies. Although the majority of group business will be booked further in advance, those rates are also determined by the revenue manager and director of sales based on historical trends and future business needs.

3. Competitor Analysis: It is always valuable to know what the competition is doing. Revenue management is part science and part craft. With the advancement in technology, Many revenue management companies have created essential tools that allow hoteliers and revenue managers to determine their position in the marketplace. They produced the report that is routed on a weekly and monthly basis. This report allows a hotel to choose a competitive set, which then compares the hotel's actualized results by segment versus the competitive set, resulting in market share indexes for occupancy, ADR, and REV PAR. Although it is every hotel's goal to capture fair market share , it is a greater priority to gain share by outperforming the competition.

4. Distribution Channels: It is crucial to know where the business is coming from, and how to increase production from the right channels. Most hotel brands have a central reservations system, which is powered by their Web site and land-based call centers. In addition, there are thousands of travel agencies that book rooms into hotels, which includes: online agencies (i.e., Expedia and Makemytrip) and land-based agencies . The major agencies will have regional market managers that will supply market share data along with insight on any future developments that could be very beneficial to a hotel's strategy. A great revenue manager will establish daily communications with the large agencies to gain knowledge and to leverage hotel placement on their Web sites. Customers will not book you if they can't find you. The same applies to land-based travel agents, which are generally serviced by the hotel's sales and marketing team, who can be great resources in looking into the future. Greater market intelligence can equate to sound decision making.

5. Pricing Strategies: There is no right and wrong to the number of times rates should be adjusted on any given night. However, a greater

understanding of market dynamics will come from a balance of historical knowledge and future market intelligence. Lastly, this question will always be asked: Could we have done something different to maximize REV PAR? It is the revenue manager's responsibility to answer the question with integrity. Successful general managers will appreciate the honesty and will have greater confidence level in a revenue manager that can determine both strengths and weaknesses in their own strategies.

CHAPTER FIFTEEN

Trends in Rooms Division Operations

• Diversity of work force. All the pundits are projecting a substantial increase in the number of women and minorities who will not only be taking hourly paid positions, but also supervising and management positions as well.

• Increase in use of technology. Reservations are being made by individuals over the Internet. Travel agents are able to make reservations at more properties. There is increasing simplification of the various PMSs and their interface with POS systems. In the guest room, increasing demand for high-speed Internet access, category 5 cables, and in some cases equipment itself is anticipated.

• Continued quest for increases in productivity. As pressure mounts from owners and management companies, hotel managers are looking for innovative ways to increase productivity and to measure productivity by sales per employee.

• Increasing use of revenue management. The techniques of revenue management will increasingly be used to increase profit by effective pricing of room inventory.

• Greening of hotels and guest rooms. Recycling and the use of environmentally friendly products, amenities, and biodegradable detergents will increase. Energy management technology is used for the reduction of energy costs by setting back temperature and shutting off power in vacant rooms through control sensors that regulate the HVA C system.

• Security. Guests continue to be concerned about personal security. - Hotels are constantly working to improve guest security. For example, one hotel has instituted a women-only floor with concierge and security. Implementation of security measures will increase.

• Diversity of the guest. More women travelers are occupying hotel rooms. This is particularly a result of an increase in business travel.

• Compliance with the ADA. As a result of the Americans with Disabilities Act (ADA), all hotels must modify existing facilities and incorporate design features into new constructions that make areas accessible to persons with disabilities. All hotels are expected to have at least four percent of their parking space designated as "handicapped." These spaces must be wide enough for wheelchairs to be unloaded from a van. Guest rooms must be fitted with equipment that can be manipulated by persons with disabilities. Restrooms must be wide enough to accommodate wheelchairs. Ramps should be equipped with handrails, and meeting rooms must be equipped with special listening systems for those with hearing impairments.

• Use of hotels' Web sites. Hotel companies will continue to try to persuade guests to book rooms using the hotel company Web site rather than via an Internet site such as Hotels.com because the hotel must pay about INR-200 for each room booking from such sites.

• In-room technology upgrades. The increase in personal devices such as smartphones, iPads, and other portable technology presents hotels with a need to facilitate the use of these devices in guestrooms. Some hotels are now offering personal iPads for use while staying in guestrooms, some of which act as the guest's personal concierge.

• Television service upgrades. The steady increase in Netflix subscribers and other streaming devices causes a need to beef up television content and offerings to guests. This has also led to a decrease in "payper-view" movies. Some hotels are offering technology featuring free HD movies and television, as well as the ability to connect to the Internet over the television screen, or through an inclusive connectivity panel, guests are able to connect their own electronic devices to their television set.

CHAPTER SIXTEEN

Security/Loss Prevention

Providing guest protection and loss prevention is essential for any lodging establishment regardless of size. Violent crime is a growing problem, and protecting guests from bodily harm has been defined by the courts as a reasonable expectation from hotels. The security/loss division is responsible for maintaining security alarm systems and implementing procedures aimed at protecting the personal property of guests and employees and the hotel itself.

A comprehensive security plan must include the following elements:

Security Officers

• These officers make regular rounds of the hotel premises, including guest floors, corridors, public and private function rooms, parking areas, and offices.

• Duties involve observing suspicious behavior and taking appropriate action, investigating incidents, and cooperating with local law enforcement agencies.

Equipment

• Two-way radios between security staff are common.

• Closed-circuit television cameras are used in out-of-the-way corridors and doorways, as well as in food, liquor, and storage areas.

• Smoke detectors and fire alarms, which increase the safety of the guests, are a requirement in every part of the hotel by law.

• Electronic key cards offer superior room security. Key cards typically do not list the name of the hotel or the room number. So, if lost or stolen, the key is not easily traceable. In addition, most key card systems record every entry in and out of the room on the computer for further reference.

Safety Procedures

• Front-desk agents help maintain security by not allowing guests to reenter their rooms once they have checked out. This prevents any loss of hotel property by guests.

• Security officers should be able to gain access to guest rooms, store rooms, and offices at all times.

• Security staff develop catastrophe plans to ensure staff and guest safety and to minimize direct and indirect costs from disaster. The catastrophe plan reviews insurance policies, analyzes physical facilities, and evaluates possible disaster scenarios, including whether they have a high or low probability of occurring. Possible disaster scenarios may include fires, bomb threats, earthquakes, floods, hurricanes, and blizzards. The well-prepared hotel develops formal policies to deal with any possible scenario and trains employees to implement chosen procedures should they become necessary.

Identification Procedures

• Identification cards with photographs should be issued to all employees.

• Name tags for employees who are likely to have contact with guests not only project a friendly image for the property, but are also useful for security reasons.

CHAPTER SEVENTEEN

Management Systems

Energy Management Systems : Technology is used to extend guest in-room comfort by means of an energy management system. Passive infrared motion sensors and door switches can reduce energy consumption by 30 percent or more by automatically switching off lights and air-conditioning, thus saving energy when the guest is out of the room. Additional features include the following:

- Room occupancy status reporting
- Automatic lighting control
- Minibar access reporting
- Smoke detector alarm reporting
- Central electronic lock control
- Guest control amenities

Because of increasing energy costs, some operators are installing software programs that will turn off nonessential equipment during the peak billing times of day (utility companies' charges are based on peak usage). Hospitality operators can save money by utilizing this type of energy-saving software to reduce their energy costs.

Call Accounting Systems

Call accounting systems (CAS) track guest room phone charges. Software packages can be used to monitor where calls are being made and from which phones on the property. To track this information, the CAS must work in conjunction with the PBX (telephone) and the PMS. Call accounting systems today can be used to offer different rates for local guest calls and long-distance guest calls. The CAS can even be used to offer discounted calling during off-peak hours at the hotel.

Guest Reservation Systems

Before hotels started using the Internet to book reservations, they received reservations by letters, telegrams, faxes, and phone calls. Airlines were the first industry to start using global distribution systems (GDS) for reservations. Global distribution systems are electronic markets for travel, hotel, car rental, and attraction bookings.

A central reservation system (CRS) houses the electronic database in the central reservation office (CRO). Hotels provide rates and availability information to the CRO usually by data communication lines. This automatically updates the CRS so that guests get the best available rate when they book through the central reservation office. Guests instantly receive confirmation of their reservation or cancellation. The hotel benefits from using a central reservation system. With such a system, hotels can avoid overselling rooms by too large a margin. The CRS database can also be used as a chain or individual property marketing tool because guest information can easily be stored. A CRS can also provide yield management information for a hotel. The more flexible a central reservation system is, the more it will help with yield management. For example, when demand is weak for a hotel, rates will need to drop to increase reservations and profitability. When demand is higher, the hotel can sell room rates that are closer to the rack rate (rack rate is the highest rate quoted for a guestroom, from which all discounts are offered).

A CRS can be used in several areas of a hotel. If a hotel has a reservations department, the terminals or personal computers in that department can be connected to the central reservation system. It is also important for front-desk employees to have access to the CRS so that they know what the hotel has available because they may need to book rooms for walkins who don't have reservations. Constant communication back and forth is needed between the central reservation system and the front-office and reservations department. Managers who are the decision makers in the hotel will also use the system to forecast and set pricing for rooms and different amenities. Hotels can use other forms of technology to facilitate reservation systems. Several companies offer an application service provider (ASP) environment that can deliver a complete booking system tied to the hotel's inventory in real time via the Web. One operator, Paul Wood of the El Dorado Hotel in Santa Fe, New Mexico, says that he simply went to the ASP Web site and put in a promotional corporate rate for the summer, and the same day he started seeing reservations coming in with that code. After a few months, bookings were up three percent over the previous year.

Billing Guests

Hospitality businesses today seek to obtain the most high-speed and reliable computer systems they can afford that they can use to bill their guests without delay. Fast access to guests' accounts is required by large hotels because of their high priority of guest satisfaction (no lineups at checkout). Billing guests has become much easier with the aid of computers. Billing guests can be a long process if information technologies are not used to complete transactions. PMSs aid large hotels to make faster transactions and provide a more efficient service to their guests. These systems help the hospitality associates bill their guests within seconds. Some hotels utilize software that enables guests to check and approve their bills by using the TV and remote control, thus avoiding the need to line up at the cashier's desk to check out. A copy of the final bill is then mailed to the guest's home address.

Security

Each business in the hospitality industry offers some sort of security for its guests and employees. Peace of mind that the hotel or restaurant is secure is a key factor in increasing guest satisfaction. Security is one of the highest concerns of guests who visit hospitality businesses. Hospitality information technology systems include surveillance systems in which cameras are installed in many different areas of the property to monitor the grounds and help ensure guest safety. These cameras are linked directly to computers, televisions, and digital recorders, which helps security teams keep an eye on the whole property. Recent technological advances have produced electronic door locking systems, some of which even offer custom configurations of security and safety. Guest room locks are now capable of managing information from both magstripe and smart cards simultaneously. From the hotel's point of view, a main advantage of this kind of key is that the hotel knows who has entered the room and at what time because the system can trace anyone entering the room. In-room safes can now be operated by key cards. Both systems are an improvement on the old metal keys. Even smarter safes use biometric technology such as the use of thumbprints or retina scans to verify a user's identity

Guest Comfort and Convenience

Hotels provide guest comfort and convenience to maintain a home-awayfrom-home feeling for their guests. Hotels receive recognition when they provide many additional in-room services and amenities for their guests, such as dining, television, telephones, Internet connections, minibars, and hygiene products. These amenities help provide a cozy experience for the guest. Many other services can be provided outside of the rooms, such as swimming pools, massages, fine dining, postal services, and meeting space. Other services are provided to suit the demands of all types of guests; a concierge and business center is one example. Hotels communicate with many entities to provide services for their guests. Some companies offer creative solutions to hotels for enhanced inroom services for guests.

CHAPTER EIGHTEEN

Technology Spotlight

"Home away from home!" This is how we would like to express what hotels mean to our guests. For this to happen, we must provide technologies that guests use at home. Of course, the main purpose of the guestroom has never changed: to provide a clean, safe place to spend the night. In 70, for the first time, hoteliers put ice-cube makers and small refrigerators inside the guestroom. In the beginning, not all rooms had these amenities. Usually, those rooms that had these special amenities were charged more than the other rooms. In 72, the first models of telephone systems were introduced to the guestroom. In those days, there was only one telephone line for the entire hotel; therefore, guests sometimes waited long hours before they could place a call. In 75, after color TV was well established in homes, hotels started to offer it. In the beginning, some hotels advertised that they had color TV to differentiate themselves from the competition and charged extra for rooms with TV. In 80, the Hotel Billing Information System (HOBIS) was introduced. In 81, it became legal for hotels to profit from phone calls. This is when call accounting systems exploded in the hotel industry. In 86, electronic door-keys were introduced, increasing the security and the convenience of guests. Interface between TV systems and property management systems were established in 1990 so that the guests could see their bills through the TV. With that, in 93, guests were able to check out from their room by using the TV. In 95, high-speed Internet access was available in hotel rooms. After 2000, hotels started to use Voice over Internet Protocol (VoIP) phoning systems, high-definition TV, wireless Internet access, interactive entertainment systems, smart-energy management systems, and many other systems. In today's modern hotel rooms, it is possible to see the following technologies that make the guest stay a more comfortable one: (1) electronic locking system, (2) energy management and climate control systems, (3) fire alarm and security systems, (4) in-room minibars, (5) in-room safe boxes, (6) guestroom phone systems, (7) voice-mail/wake-up systems, (8) in-room entertainment systems, (9) guestroom control panels, and (10) self check-in/check-out systems.

Let's look into the future to see what the guestroom might look like: You just booked a hotel room from your smartphone with a voice command. When you go to check in to the hotel, you see that check-in desk is replaced with a "hospitality desk." As soon as you arrive at the hotel, your phone is showing you a map of the hotel rooms, asking you to make a choice. Once you make your choice, your phone becomes your electronic key card. When you wave your phone, the door opens and the 100-percent sustainable room welcomes you with your preferred wall color (thanks to nanopaint) and your favorite song. When you turn on the TV with your voice command, you see your favorite and local TV channels (thanks to Internet TV) and your video library from your home phone. The picture frame shows the pictures from your Facebook page. Your sheets and towels will be changed based on "green" preferences, such as to change the bed sheets and towels every three days and bring the temperature of the room 10 degrees down or up based on the season when you are not in the room. When you need help, you connect to a virtual concierge to get any kind of information about the hotel and the area. The wardrobe door generates power when you open and close the door for lighting. When you use the restroom, the smart toilet checks your health and sends you a digital report to your e-mail. Actually, this is a description of a nextgeneration hotel.

Sustainable Lodging

Green Hotel Initiatives

The environmentally conscious companies are not only helping to avoid further environmental degradation but are also saving themselves money while being good corporate citizens. Operationally, hotels have been recycling for years and saving water and chemicals by leaving cards in guest rooms saying that sheets will be changed every third day unless otherwise requested. Some hotels move the top sheet down to the bottom on the second or third day. Likewise, a card in the bathroom explains to guests that if they want a towel changed to leave it on the floor. Hotels have been quick to realize that the life of sheets and towels has been greatly extended, thus increasing savings.

The wattage of lighting has been reduced and long-life and florescent bulbs are saving thousands of dollars a year per property. Air-conditioning units can now control the temperature of a room through body-motion sensing devices that even pick up people's breathing. These devices can automatically shut off the air-conditioning unit when guests are out of their rooms. Savings are also being made with low-flow toilets and showerheads that have high-pressure, low-volume flows of water. Ecoefficiency, also generally termed green, is based on the concept of creating more goods and services while using fewer resources and creating less waste and pollution. In other words, it means doing more with less. So what does this have to do with your bottom line? Ecoefficiency helps hotels provide better service with fewer resources; reducing the materials and energy-intensity of goods and services lowers the hotel's ecological impact and improves the bottom line. It's a key driver for overall business performance.

Triple bottom line, sometimes called the TBL or 3P approach (people, planet, and profits), requires thinking in three dimensions, not one. It takes into account ecological and societal performance in addition to financial.

Today, quantifiable environmental impacts include consumption of finite resources, energy usage, water quality and availability, and pollution emitted. Social impacts include community health, employee and guest safety, education quality, and diversity.

Being green is also financially good for certified properties. By saving energy and water, reducing waste, and eliminating toxic chemicals, green properties lower their operating costs, which allows them to provide enhanced services to their guests and a healthier environment for both their guests and employees. Sustainable properties are doing the following to become more sustainable in their operating practices:

Reducing energy needs by doing the following:

- Installing motion sensors in public areas and occupancy sensors in guestrooms
- Installing energy-efficient lighting, dimmers, and timers to reduce energy consumption
- Installing LED (light-emitting diode) exit signs
- Installing Energy Star appliances
- Increasing building insulation
- Using natural day lighting whenever possible
- Tightening the property shell, with added/better insulation, eliminating leaks, replacing windows

Conserving water by doing the following:

- Installing aerators on faucets
- Installing water diverters on existing toilets or installing low-flow toilets
- Installing low-flow showerheads
- Implementing towel and linen reuse programs
- Landscaping with native plants
- Using timers/moisture sensors in landscape watering
- Changing lawn watering to encourage deeper root growth

Reducing waste by doing the following:

- Providing recycling areas for guests and staff
- Purchasing postconsumer recycled paper and buying in bulk
- Serving meals with cloth napkins and reusable china and dinnerware

- Using refillable soap/shampoo dispensers in bathrooms
- Recycling usable furniture and other items at "dump stores" or through charity
- Reusing old towels and linens as cleaning rags
- Asking vendors to minimize packaging Recycling cooking grease
- Composting food and lawn waste

Reducing hazardous waste by doing the following:

- Properly disposing of fluorescent lighting, computers, and other electronic equipment
- Participating in local hazardous waste collection days
- Using low-VOC (volatile organic compound) paints, carpets, and glues
- Using rechargeable batteries
- Using energy-efficient shuttle vans
- Using environmentally friendly cleaning products

CHAPTER TWENTY

Handling guest queries

The front office is the main point of contact for all guests, so it is here that most of the queries and requests are directed. The concierge, porters and doorman all assist in this area by responding to guest queries. Often the guest will talk to reception about the particular query and reception will contact other departments within the hotel to assist with these queries. The opportunity to describe facilities may occur at any time during a guest's stay. As a receptionist you are required to know about all areas of the property, from food and beverage to housekeeping and business center services. That is a lot of information to absorb, and items such as restaurant opening hours will be constantly changing, so you must ensure your knowledge is up to date.

Guest queries

In the Hospitality Industry, remember that the guest is the reason you work, not an interruption to it. If there were no guests, you would not have a job. You are in a service industry and your job is to give good service. When a guest asks questions, you must never think of it as an inconvenience. React promptly, give the guest your full attention and show genuine interest in their questions.

If you know the answer:

• Tell the guest and ask if there is anything else you can help them with

• Finish the conversation with a pleasant greeting, e.g. 'I hope you enjoy your stay'.

If you don't know the answer:

• Never make it up or say, 'I don't know' or 'That's not my department'

• Offer to find out and get back to the guest with the answer

• Do not keep the guest waiting while you try to find the answer

• Make sure you follow up and get back to the guest quickly.

Involvement of other departments

Handling guest queries might involve communication with other departments and it is vital to establish and maintain good communication with these departments Departments that may be involved include:
- Concierge

- Messages and mail delivery
- Requests regarding booking tickets to venues and entertainment
- Tour bookings
- Hire cars
- Handle all bookings and arrangements for facilities outside the hotel.

- Housekeeping

- Extra facilities in the room such as blankets, pillows and towels, baby goods, even an extra bed
- Unlock connecting doors
- Extra service of a room

- Room Service

- Arrange for food or beverage orders to be delivered to the room

- Maintenance

- To fix any faults in the room, for example; light bulb on the bedside lamp is broken or air conditioning isn't working properly

- Restaurants, Bars and other outlets

- Make reservations for the hotel guests
- Report any food allergies or special requests

CHAPTER TWENTY-ONE

Handling customer concerns and objections

Handling Guest Complaints

1. Approach the complaining guest politely as you say: "Anything I can do for you or May I help you sir?"

2. Listen attentively; let him finish his statement before reacting. If the message is not clear, confirm or clarify.

"if I got you right sir, are you saying that..."

"I heard you say.... Do you mean that........

3. Get more details:

Guest: Your service is lousy.

Steward: What exactly went wrong sir?

Could you recall the name of the staff?

4. Be calm and sober even if the customer is rude or shouting at the peak of his voice. Be gracious and courteous no matter how irritating the customer is.

5. Be open minded; accept the facts of his complaints and refrain from being defensive. Acknowledge customer comments even if he does not seem to be talking sense.

"I see your point sir"

"I understand what you mean."'

"Your comment is well taken sir."

"I have taken note of your complaint sir."

6. Accept the customer's feeling, saying something like:

"I can understand how you feel."

"I can see how irritated you are and I understand why you feel that way."

If the customer is very upset, mad or irritated, pacify the guest by saying the magic words like:

"What can I do to make you feel better?" or

"What can we do to compensate for our deficiency?"

7. Never argue nor disagree or indiscreetly prove the customer wrong. If the comment

is an unsound accusation, raise your point by acknowledging the comments first

before presenting your point.

"I can see that you are not satisfied with our ______________ and I respect your

comments. However, I am quite surprised because that item happens to be our most

saleable one."

8. If service is faulty, apologize. Say "I am sorry for what happened."

9. Settle sensitive matters or problems in private so as not place the customer in an

embarrassing situation.

Examples: declined credit card, shortage of cash for payment and suspended signing

privilege.

These situations should be referred to the supervisor who will ask his staff to request

the customer to see him in a private office or away from the view of other customers

or staff.

The service staff will tell the customer

"Excuse me sir, someone wish to see you at the counter."

Do not say: "my supervisor is calling for you."

10. Never pass the blame on another person or department in an effort to defend oneself.

11. If the customer is very upset and does not want to accept apologies or is making a fuss out of petty matters or cannot be pacified, call the supervisor or manager.

12. Should a complaint or request require a delicate decision or action, or a request that run counter to some business policies like discount or waiving service charge, etc.

refer to the supervisor.

13. The clerk should tell the customer: "im sorry sir but I am not authorized to decide on this matter, may I refer you to my supervisor?"

14. Take appropriate action immediately and assure the complaining customer that his concern is being taken seriously and that corrective action shall be taken.

15. When the customer is exhibiting scandalous behaviour like shouting or uttering provocative statements alert the security officer and get security assistance especially when violent reactions are already displayed. However, the security officer must be discreet in dealing with the customer.

Before any security personnel takes over, the supervisor must try to pacify the customer first, get him away from the lounge or service area and talk to him in private.

16. Show appreciation rather than irritation upon receiving a complaint or negative remark.

"Thank you, sir, for bringing this matter to our attention,"

Front Office Operation | Course File

"I have taken note of your comments sir. Thank you for calling our attention. We will see to it that it won't happen again.

CHAPTER TWENTY-TWO

COMMUNICATIONS

The communication plays a vital role in proper co-ordination of each section, divisions of the hotel to perform as a separate entity. Each department of the hotel needs to share lots of information among themselves to carry out their day to day functions. An ambiguous communication may lead to a miserable situation; therefore, communication should be precise and clear.

Communication Process

Communication is defined as process by which people seek to share meaning through the transmission of the symbolic messages. Term process refers to identifiable flow of information through interrelated stages of analysis directed towards the achievement of an objective. The entire communication process may be broken into various elements of communication like sender, message, encoding, channel, receiver, decoding, and feedback.

Source (the sender of the message): Source of the message is the person who wishes to share the information, facts or feelings with another person or group of peoples (the target audience of the message). In context to hospitality industry, the sender of the message may be subordinate, peer, and superior who wishes to pass information to one or more target audience of the message.

Message: Message is the subject matter of the communication that is passed from sender to target audience. It may be a views, ideas, feelings, orders, recommendations, facts, data, request, etc.

Encoding: The subject matter of communication is nonfigurative and intangible, its transmission requires use of symbols like words, gestures, photo etc. the process of converting the abstract ideas into communication symbols is called encoding.

Channel: The way through which the encoded message passes is known as channels of communication. It may use any channel like written form, telephonic conversation, personal contact etc. the channel of communication depends upon the situation of the sender and the receiver.

Target (the receiver of the message): Target is the person to whom the message is sent by the sender. The receiver of the message may be the peer, senior or subordinate.

Decoding: Decoding is the converting the encoded symbols into abstract ideas. It is a reversal of the encoding. By doing so the target receives the original message.

Feedback: Feedback ensures that the target has received the message and understands the message in the same sense as it was intended by the sender.

Importance of communication

Communication is very important for proper co-ordination among the various department of the organisation. Every department of the hotel shares information from each other for proper planning and execution of the task performed by them. The front office department of the hotel communicates with the other department like housekeeping for status of rooms and at the same time housekeeping will require the information about the day's arrival, expected VIP, group; to schedule the requirement of the employees for smooth operation of the department. The importance of communication is as under:

• Essential for planning
• Essential for decision making
• Essential for effective co-ordination

Essential for planning: A good planning requires lots of information. The organisation gathers information from each sections or department through the communication. The planning will be sound if we are able to gather quality and relevant information. The better communication helps to generate the required information for planning.

Essential for decision making: Decision making is an indispensable component of management process. Decision making is choosing the best alternative from the available options. One requires studying all available options before choosing the most suitable alternatives. The managers are getting all necessary information form organisation through communication. Hence effective communication plays a vital role in decision making process.

Essential for effective co-ordination: Co-ordination among the departments is the key factor in providing flawless services to hotel guests. The effective co- ordination is achieved though proper communication among the departments of the hotel.

Oral and written communication

Words are the most common symbols of communication. In oral communication, both the parties to the communication exchange their ideas through oral words either in face-to-face communication or through electronic devices like telephone etc. the oral communication is easy, effective, and produces instant feedback from the other party to communication. Oral communication has limitations like lack of proof, lack of authenticity, and time consuming even though employees are spending a substantial part of their time in oral communication. Written communication is in the form of letters, circulars, notes, manuals, house magazines etc. The written communication has its own merits like authenticity and proof for future reference and suffers demerits like over formalization, cost, and lack secrecy.

Barriers of communication

Communication breakdown is cited as major problem by the managers. The problem of communication arises because there are various obstacles which may entirely prevent a communication, filter a part of it out, or give an incorrect meaning. These obstacles are known as barriers of communication. The barriers of communication may be grouped as semantic barriers, psychological barriers, organizational barriers, and personal barriers.

Interdepartmental communication

Front office department plays a pivotal role in delivering quality services to the guest. The front office manager must take an active role in gathering information of interest to guests and in developing procedures for the front office to use in disbursing this information. The efficient functioning of an organisation requires a close coordination and cooperation between the departments or sub- sections. The effective coordination is attained by proper and accurate communication.

Housekeeping: Front office and Housekeeping department communicates with each other for the information as under:

? Room Status

? Security Concerns

? Special Arrangements

Room Status: Room is the most perishable commodity sold by the hotel. Hence a tight control over the room status is mandatory to run a profitable hotel business. The Front office department and Housekeeping must closely coordinate on the Room status. Housekeeping department prepares an Occupancy report which is sent to front office department where is tallied with room status records of front desk to find any discrepancy. This helps to:

- Update room status
- Find sleepers (A room from which guest has already checked out but it is shown occupied in front office room status records)
- Know the exact house count.
- Charge guest if extra person has occupied the room.
- Coordinates in guest room change.

Security Concerns: The front desk needs information from housekeeping personnel regarding any unusual circumstances which may indicate a violation of security for the hotel guests. For example, if a house keeping person notices obviously non registered guest on a floor, sounds of domestic disturbances in a guest room, a fire exit that has been propped open or any other unusual events. The front desk personnel after receiving such information will inform in house or civil authorities so that guest security concern is not harmed.

Special Arrangements: The guest may request for additional or special amenities during their stay like extra blanket, towel, soap, shampoo, iron, oil etc. When such requests are received at front desk, it should be immediately relayed to the housekeeping department. Some time front office may also request housekeeping department to put extra amenities in the guest room like flower arrangement, bath robe etc. The front desk also informs housekeeping department to make special arrangements for:

- VIP's in house.
- Groups in house
- Crew in house.

Food and Beverage Department: The front office department coordinates with food and beverage department for smooth functioning of hotel. The front office department sends information to food and beverage department which helps them to plan their work schedule and staff requirement to carry out day to day function of the department. The front desk sends information like:

- Arrival and departure notification of guest.
- Bar set up in VIP room
- Special arrangement like cookies, fruit basket and assorted dry fruits
- VIP and corporate guest in house
- Groups expected and Groups in house
- Crew in house
- All payment cash notification at point of sales for scanty baggage in-house guest.
- Arrangement for food and beverages for the groups and guests staying on meal plan.

Sales and marketing department: The front office department coordinates with sales and marketing department for information like:

- Guest histories
- Room reservation records
- Current room availability status
- Group, corporate and crew bookings
- Setting the transient and bulk room sales

This information helps both the department to sell the highly perishable hospitality product- The hotel room. The front office staff must take every effort to keep the data base like room availability status, guest histories etc. current and accurate. The marketing and sales executives may have to check the list of available rooms three; six or even twelve months in future to be sure that hotel can accommodate the expected number of guest. This information helps sales and marketing department to sell hotel products by bundling more than two hospitality products like rooms with meals, rooms with meals and entertainment leading to hospitality sales in totality. Therefore a close cooperation and coordination between the two departments is important.

Engineering and Maintenance: The front office communicates with engineering and maintenance department for proper upkeep of equipments and systems installed in the department as well as in the rooms. The front office informs any maintenance require in the department. In case if maintenance activity require in a room already occupied by a guest, the two departments work out a time frame so that maintenance should be carried out off sight of the guest or room may be changed. The request from guest to repair equipments and systems installed in room may also be routed through front desk. In case such request is received at front desk it is transferred to maintenance department and a feedback should also be taken from maintenance as guest may want to be informed when the repair may be made.

Security: The front office in a hotel is a vital link between management of the hotel and the guest. When a guest calls for assistance because of security concerns like fire, ill ness, and theft other emergency, it is usually the front desk that must respond. The front desk personnel cannot leave the station to resolve the guest problem as they must continue to provide communication services and process financial transactions. In that case front desk sends the security personnel on duty to resolve the guest problems.

Controller: The front desk communicates with controller to provide a daily summary of financial transactions after night auditing. The information provided by the front desk helps the controller to make budgets and allocate finance for the current financial period. The front desk provide the controller the financial data for billing and maintenance of credit card ledgers, high balance reports etc. enables the controller to formulate policy guidelines and strategies to recover the money from the guests and companies.

Human Resource: A close coordination and communication between front desk and human resource division is a secret of successful functioning of the front office department. The front desk informs:

- About the requirement of staff.
- Training requirement for the staff.
- Refresher training for the staff.
- Cross training requirement.
- Multi skilling.

These information help human resource department to develop guidelines for initial screening of candidates to get the quality personnel for front desk. The guidelines may include concerns about personal hygiene, completion of application, education requirement, citizenship status, and experience.

Banquets: The front office department coordinates with banquets for putting information on bulletin board and placing directional signals for particular function area. The guest attending the function who is unfamiliar with the hotel may ask for directions at front desk. The banquet department sends function prospectus to front desk so that if any communication from the parties to function lands at front desk may be transferred or replied promptly. The preparation of marquee with congratulatory, welcome, sales promotion or important messages is handled by the front desk employee if such activity is required by the host of the party should be informed to the front desk through the banquet manger, so that it should be handled efficiently.

CHAPTER TWENTY-THREE

TELEPHONE MANNERS

QUALITIES TO TRANSMIT

FRIENDLINESS - Your voice will carry your attitude over the phone.

CONFIDENCE - Prepare yourself. This will enable you to speak with confidence. Know your property. Know how to analyze your status data quickly.

INTELLIGENCE - Remember that you are talking with individuals from different backgrounds
and levels of education. Meet your caller on his level.

CLARITY - It is embarrassing for the listener to ask you to repeat a statement.

CREATIVENESS - If the opportunity avails itself, help solve problems. Use your expertise to offer alternatives he may not have thought of.

ENTHUSIASM - Find out the positive points about your property and concentrate on them.

INTEGRITY - Be honest, If you do not know, admit it & offer to find out. Do not mislead your prospect.

TACTFULNESS - Be tactful in any situation. Try to convince the guest without hurting his feelings.

PRIDE - Take pride in your company and your work. Let the pride reflect in your voice and your speech. Pride generates enthusiasm. Your pride in the hotel will instill interest & confidence in the mind of the caller.

USE OF TELEPHONE BY FRONT OFFICE STAFF

1. The telephone is to be used for reception business. If you want to make a private call, use the private call box in the lobby. If somebody telephones you personally (not on business), keep your conversation as brief as possible and offer to telephone back from the call box when you are free. Unless you do this, you may keep waiting a potential guest who wants to make a booking.

2. When the telephone rings answer it immediately. The call should be attended within three rings. If you are attending to a guest at that time, first answer the phone, excuse yourself. Do not let the telephone ring without answering it. Although it may at times be irritating the telephone should always come before any desk work, but should not take precedence over the guest at the counter with whom you were dealing before the telephone rang.

3. Do not keep the caller waiting for a long time before attending to him.
A caller on the telephone should never be left longer than 45 seconds without somebody picking up the telephone and telling him again "I am sorry to keep you waiting."

4. Answer the telephone by saying, "RECEPTION (inf. or reservation) GOOD MORNING (good afternoon or good evening), MAY I HELP YOU? Do not answer "Hello".

5. Speak clearly. Pronounce the words carefully. The caller may find it more difficult to understand you on the telephone than if you speak to him at the counter.

6. Be brief and to the point, but not abrupt. Remember that telephone time costs money and that the switchboard operator may be holding another call for you.

7. Be polite, friendly and helpful. On the telephone only your voice can indicate the welcome we want every potential guest to receive. Do not interrupt the caller while he is talking. You must never sound short, sharp, irritated and impatient.

8. Be accurate in what you say. The guest wants to have confidence in you. Do not 'THINK' or 'SUPPOSE' if you do not know the answer; find out and call back.

9. Be courteous in explaining the hotel rules. Do not use the phrase "You have to", "I suggest" or "would you mind" is preferable. Never argue with the guest, the guest is always right. If you can not deal with a certain problem, inform the seniors in the department, so that they can deal with it.

10. Take the correct name and contact number of the caller. This information will help you if you have telephone the caller back.

11. Finally, Always remember that you represent the hotel or the organisation you are working for when you pick-up a telephone call at work. Caller does not see you or your hotel, so your voice alone has to help the caller become and remain a satisfied customer.

Telephone Etiquette

Before you answer be prepared (this includes knowing how to use the phone/system features):

1. Turn away from your computer, desk or other work.

2. Have pens, pencils and notepaper handy.

In answering the phone:

3. Answer calls promptly, by the second or third ring.

4. Smile as you pick up the phone.

5. Assume your "telephone" voice, controlling your volume and speed.

6. Project a tone that is enthusiastic, natural, attentive and respectful.

7. Greet the caller and identify yourself and your company/department/ unit.

8. Ask, "To whom am I speaking?"

9. Ask, "How may I help you?"

In the course of the conversation:

10. Focus your entire attention on the caller.

11. Enunciate/articulate clearly. Speak distinctly.

12. Use Plain English and avoid unnecessary jargon and acronyms.

13. Use action specific words and directions.

14. Use the caller's name during the conversation.

15. Always speak calmly and choose your words naturally.

16. Use all of your listening skills:

a. Focus your full attention on the caller and the conversation.

b. Listen "between" the words.

c. Use reflective/active listening to clarify and check for understanding.

17. If there is a problem, project a tone that is concerned, empathetic, and apologetic.

18. Avoid the Five Forbidden Phrases.

a. "I don't know"

Instead, say: "That is a good question; let me find out for you" or offer to connect the caller with someone who could provide the answer.

If a call involves some research, assure the person that you will call back by a specific time.

If you do not have an answer by the deadline, call back to say, "I don't have an answer yet, but I'm still researching it." There is no excuse for not returning calls.

b. "I/we can't do that." Instead say: "This is what I/we can do."

c. "You'll have to" Instead say: "You will need to" or "I need you to" or "Here's how we can help you."

d. "Just a second" Instead: Give a more honest estimate of how long it will take you and/or let them know what you are doing.

e. "No." Instead: Find a way to state the situation positively.

19. Use "LEAPS" with the emotional caller to vent.

L Listen; allow the caller to vent.

E Empathize; acknowledge the person's feelings

A Apologize when appropriate, even if the problem is not your fault, you can say, "I am really sorry this has happened" and mean it.

P (Be) Positive

S Solve; suggest/generate solutions that you can both agree on and/or ask what you can do to help and, if reasonable, do it! If not, find a compromise.

In concluding the call:

20. End the conversation with agreement on what is to happen next; if you are to follow-up, do so immediately.

21. Thank the caller for calling; invite the caller to call again.

In transferring calls:

22. Transfer ONLY when necessary; get the information yourself.

23. If you must transfer, avoid the use of the word "transfer." Say instead: "I am going to connect you with".

24. Explain why you are "transferring" the call.

25. Give the caller the person's name and direct number

26. Stay on the line and introduce the caller.

In taking messages:

27. Identify yourself and for whom you are answering the phone.

28. Practice political sensitivity.

29. Indicate the period of time the person will be unavailable.

30. Write down all the important information given:

a. The name of the caller. Ask for spelling if unclear.

b. The (correct) telephone number of the caller.

c. The message. Ask for clarification if necessary.

31. Read back what you've written to be sure you've understood the message correctly.

32. Always assure the person that you will deliver the message promptly.

33. Deliver the message in a timely fashion.

NEVER:

34. Eat, drink or chew gum while on the phone.

35. Leave an open line:

a. Place the caller on hold

b. Check back with the caller frequently: every 30-45 seconds.

ALWAYS:

36. Put a smile in your telephone voice and let your personality shine!

The Complaint Call

Complaint callers who are irate are really saying, "I rate." They have bought into society's "the squeaky

wheel gets the grease" mentality. When that happens, try the EAR method:

E mpathize with the caller.

A pologize and acknowledge the problem.

Accept R esponsibility. (You'll do something.)

Empathize with the caller. This is different from sympathy, where you take on someone else's problem.

Try to understand how the person is feeling.

Apologize and acknowledge the problem. You don't have to agree with the caller, but express regret that there is a problem. People want to be heard, and no one's complaint is trivial.

Each deserves prompt handling, so do not deal with it in a trivial manner.

Accept responsibility. Make sure something is done. Take it upon yourself to DO something.

Many times, that's all that people want: the reassurance that something will be done. People want to be helped. They want to know that you care.

Use these phrases to get that sentiment across: "How can I help you?" "What can I do for you?" "I'll make sure this message/information gets to the right person."

The acceptance of responsibility may be as simple as forwarding the call to the appropriate individual or sending the caller more information.

If you do forward the caller to someone else on your staff, follow up with that person to make sure the caller was taken care of.

If you get an irate caller, or even one who is calm, cool, and collected, here are some more methods to handle complaint calls:

First, don't overreact, especially if the caller starts using "trigger" words or phrases, such as: "I want to talk to someone who knows something." Most people respond by getting defensive when their "hot-button words" are pressed.

Remember, a positive attitude is the most important asset you have.

Second, listen completely to the complaint. Allow the caller the opportunity to vent some frustration.

When you listen, don't try to apply logic to the situation. Many people are beyond logic if they are angry, so accept the feelings being expressed. Avoid argument and criticism.

Third, do not blame anyone -- the caller, yourself, or someone on your staff -- even if you know who is to blame for a problem. This information should not be shared with the caller.

Fourth, paraphrase the caller's comments, and ask questions if you do not understand the information being presented to you. Restate the problem as you understand it.

Fifth, offer solutions and, if appropriate, offer alternatives. Providing alternatives empowers callers. It gives callers a feeling that they were not dictated to and that they were part of the solution.

Finally, confirm the solution with the caller. Make sure the caller agrees with what has been decided.

Of course, not everyone will be happy, no matter what you do. These people will not be content; they just like being grumpy. Usually, these are the people who want to talk to the person "above you." If that is what it takes to lessen their anger, then do so. By the time they have been transferred to a supervisor, they usually have become calmer and less demanding. It seems that they just needed to vent their anger at someone: you. Just remember that most people are not that way and keep a firm grip on that positive attitude of yours.

Answering Telephone in Hotel & Restaurant: DOs & DON'Ts

Telephone always plays a significant role in hospitality industry. People from all round the world call for making booking or asking information or transferring message to the guest or for various other purposes. If you are a hotelier then you may have to answer telephone calls. This happens mostly with front desk staffs. Today we will learn some most effective telephone answering tips. These are some basic techniques you should apply while answering any call in hotel or restaurant.

DOs:

Answer the telephone promptly within 3 rings.

Make the caller know your work area, your name and offer appropriate greeting. If it is an inbound call then just mention your department and if it is outbound call then mention name of the hotel with your identity.

Always have pen and paper on hand, specially front desk personnel should always be ready to keep records.

Listen carefully. Pay close attention to details being expressed by the caller.

Make the caller feel that they have your undivided attention. Make an occasional acknowledgment of what he/she says. Mention the name of the caller, once established.

If you have to ask the caller to hold on, explain why. Wait for the caller's agreement before actually putting him/her on hold.

If you have to transfer the call, explain why and make sure that the caller is properly introduced to the next party. If the purpose of the call has been said already, repeat the same to the next party.

If you say you will call back, do so as soon as possible. Give him some sorts of idea that how long he or she need to wait.

Sometimes you may not understand whether the caller is a man or lady. To be on the safe side politely ask his or her name or you can say "how should i address you"?

Repeat back any details and follow up in writing (if necessary).

Close conversation politely. Always say "thank you for calling."

Let's caller hang up first.

Try to satisfy your guest with proper information. If you don't know detail then

transfer the call to the right person. Never give wrong information.

DON'Ts:

Let the telephone ring more than 3 times.

Answer the phone with merely "hello" or "yes".

Ask the caller to hold on while you scramble for pen and paper.

Rely on your memory instead of writing what the caller says. Asking the caller to repeat the details is annoying and does not leave a good impression.

Say "hold on" and leave the caller wondering if he/she is still being attended

Say "I'll transfer your call" without saying to whom and why.

Say you will call back when you have no intention to.

Say you cannot help and not offer to connect the caller to someone who can.

Say "he hasn't come in yet", "she hasn't come back from lunch yet" or "he is in the toilet".

People do not want to know the reason and are given the wrong impression by such answers.

Hang up without trying to close the conversation.

Hang up without thanking the caller for calling.

Put your least intelligent, least coherent or "panicky" staff in charge of the phone.

Keep talking to another person while answering phone.

Eating something while answering phone.

Globally used common telephonic spelling codes:

How to Take Reservation on Phone

Telephone plays an important role in times of reservation on phone.

Perfect telephone handling ensures efficiency of the reservation agent which at the same time upholds hotel's standard.

All the time you should follow proper telephone manner. These are some basic tips you should follow while you are taking reservation on phone.

Pick up the phone before 3 rings.

Greet the caller. Try to keep very fresh, clear and friendly voice tone so that guest from other side of the phone may feel comfortable. Remember First Impression is the Last Impression.

It is advisable to greet in this way "Namaskar Reservations. How may I Assist you?"

Try to identify caller gender by his or her sound. Listen to the name properly. Repeat the name with Mr. or Ms. Caller may be hurt if you by mistake call him wrongly.

Try to understand why the caller calls. In a hotel people call not only for making reservation but also for getting information, arranging party, sending message to a guest or making business deal etc. So, first listen carefully to identify what sorts of assistance the caller wants from you.

If the caller calls for room reservation and if he is not a repeated guest then you should try to give a short overview on your hotel including hotel's feature and amenities, specialty, special offer you are offering etc.

In the meantime, look at the room status or reservation chart. It will be so bad if after informing everything, guest becomes convinced and wants to have a room booked but you don't find any room to sell as all are occupied. So, always be updated specially about room status.

If callers requested date indicates "SOLD OUT" which means you are unable to sell the room for that specific date, then very politely say sorry to the guest and let him know why you are unable to sell the room.

If the requested date indicates "WAIT-LISTED" then politely inform the guest about the situation and inform him that reservation on that day is wait-listed for that reason you are taking his reservation but not giving full guarantee and request him to check again closer to that requested date.

After giving an overview of you hotel, now try to identify what sorts of room the caller wants and try to offer him some options so that he can decide from his own or if he needs then assist him.

If the guest want to book the room then say that we are very pleased to reserve a room for you. May I have some information from you please? Now try to collect these information with proper spelling:

Name of the Guest

His Contact Address

Room Types

Room Rates

Date of Arrival

Date of Departure

Date of Reservation Made

Mode of Payment

Special Remark (if any)

Reservation Made by Person or Company

Repeat all the information caller gives and at the same time give him a reservation confirmation number.

If you have any objection about guest's mode of payment or anything then inform the guest about your rules and request him to give you another option.

After settling everything thanks the caller for his patience and calling you. End up the call as warmly as you start and try to make him feel that he just have made a perfect decision.

Making Room Reservation on Telephone (SOP)

Discussion: For a front desk or reservation agent making proper reservation is the most important job. Generally most of the reservation has been done by phone. Here you will learn exactly what steps a front desk agent needs to follow to make a reservation in phone.

Steps You Should Follow:

Step-1: Answer the telephone within 3 rings.

Step-2: Greet the guest properly.

"Namaskar,Hotel ABC Hotel How may I assist you?"

Step-3: In this stage be sure about the name and when guest wants to check in and check out.

Try to understand this conversation:

Guest: "I want to make a reservation"

Agent: Ok sir. How should I address you?

Guest: I am X.

Agent: Ok Mr. X, Sir/ Madam you are from which company?

Step-4: After confirming about guest proceed to the next level. In this case, first look for room inventory. You may either find any vacant room or no room for sale. Now, follow these steps in those cases.

If you don't find any room Available:

Agent: I am terribly sorry, Mr. ABC. All our rooms are booked on XXX date. If you wish then I can put your reservation on waiting list or would you like me to recommend another hotel?

Now if guest want his reservation to be put on waiting list then take full details about the guest and give him a reservation confirmation number.

If you find a room Available:

Now your approach will be to know which room will best match with guest.

Follow these steps:

Agent: OK, MR. X, will you travel alone or not?

(As a agent your duty is to recommend such room which match with guest.

If guest travel with family then you cannot recommend him a single room and on the other hand if he comes with a family or friends then you should look for family room or others which is for more than 1 person.)

Agent: MR. X, currently we have deluxe room, suit and studio room to accommodate your family.

(If you have different types of rooms vacant then give some options to guest.)

Step-5: Try to highlight different features of each type of rooms and their price. If there any is any discounted offer, offer it. Be ready all the time for up selling.

Step-6: Make reservation properly. First be sure about guest name.

Agent: How should I spell your name sir?

Guest: It is x-.. and Then

Agent: Is it .....Then ...... ?

Guest: Yes, you are right.

Then politely request him for guaranteed booking.

Agent: Mr. X as you know our hotel is a busy hotel. So, I would like to recommend you to guarantee your booking as we have very high occupancy rate, you know.

Step-7: Explain your procedure for guaranteed reservation.

Agent: Mr. X I just make your reservation guaranteed. This will ensure your booking. Now, if you do not come on XXX date, without informing us then one night room rate will be charged from your credit card as penalty. But if you like to change your reservation then you have to inform us 24 hours in advanced. I guess you understand our policy.

Step-8: Get contact details.

Agent: May I have your contract number and address, please.

Step-9: Offer more services to your guest.

Agent: Mr. X we are offering more for our guest. Would you like us to arrange pick up service for you in the airport?

Guest: Yes, that's great.

Step-10: Now you will approach to close down the selling. Repeat all required information to be sure that you have made proper reservation.

Agent: So, Mr. X now I am going to repeat your reservation details. You like to be checking in on XXX and your checking out date is XXX. You preferred non-smoking, twin bed supreme room for you and your family. Room rent is XXX per night which included complimentary breakfast and Transfers. or You also pay in advanced for transportation service. Your confirmation number is XXX"

Guest: Yes, you are right.

Step-11: Thanks the guest for his calling and finish the conversation.

Agent: Thanks you Mr. X for choosing XXX hotel. Certainly you take the right decision. So, Mr. X see you on XXX. Have a nice day.

Agent: Ok Sir. For transportation facility, both fax or telephone and credit card guarantees are required. Once we received confirmation from you, our concierge will contact you and make all the arrangements.

Wake-up call Handling Procedure:

Wake up call is an in-house telephone call to a sleeping guest at a specific time to wake him up, predetermined by the guest. It is generally done in the morning but a guest may require any time of the day.

It is the duty of telephone department to wake up the guest but if the call will be made up for airline crews or group of guests then lobby personal will take get calls from local airline operators about the timing of the flight and then they should forward the message to telephone operator.

In case of airline crews or groups generally the wake-up call should be done 45 minutes or 1 hour before the pickup time. In small hotels it is the duty of front desk agent to wake-up guests. Here are some tips you should follow:

Give full attention to write proper room number, name and time to wake-up guest to avoid any mistake.

Always insure that guest really wakes up after your call. You can politely ask the guest that if he wants to have a 2nd wake-up call or not.

If no reply is done by the guest while you are calling or guest just hang up the phone and hardly give any reply then you should call him again.

While calling you should start this way, "Good Morning, Mr. X. This is 6 AM in the morning which is your wake up time. Have a nice day."

After getting your call, a guest may not understand the situation quickly as he just wakes up. So give him some time and explain again why you call him.

If after 2nd call, guest does not respond at all then send the bell person to knock his door and wake him up.

Proper Telephone Manner in Hotel:

Telephone plays a very important role in hotel industry. Generally people outside from hotel calls for reservation or booking or change of schedule or passing message knowing information or talking to any guest.

In all the cases the person who will receive the phone has to consider some basic telephone manner.

Also if you are a front desk agent then you have to know some telephonic spelling codes used globally to write proper spelling of a guest.

So if you are a non-English or even an English speaker you should know some well-known telephone manners.

Tips for using telephone in Hotel:

Let the caller know who you are and from where you are talking by let him know your name, your department name, designation you are holding etc.

Use some common phrases over telephone.

If you have to receive phone call frequently then you must have to have some essential materials like telephone guide, essential number and price list of your hotel, notepad, pen, pencil, eraser etc.

Try not to make the conversation lengthy, make it short and be specific

If possible try to ask some questions to know what guest want to inform that will ensure your sincerity to guest.

As over telephone no one can see each other so set your voice tone in a friendly manner.

You must not engage with other work like eating, drinking or writing while talking to guest because that could be an obstacle.

Remember and must use globally used common telephonic spelling codes.

CHAPTER TWENTY-FOUR

Glossary

Access time – the amount of time required for a processor to retrieve information from the hard drive; recorded in milliseconds. Account payable – Financial obligations the hotel owes to private and government-related agencies and vendors. Account receivable – Amount of money owed to the hotel by guests. Accountability – A manager's acceptance of the responsibility that accompanies authority and the need to justify his or her actions to higher-level managers in the organisation

Action plan – An outline of the tasks to be completed for each step in a critical path.

Agenda – A written plan for a meeting that indicates the date, time, and place for the meeting and the issues to be addressed.

Ageing of account – Indication of the stage of the payment cycle such as 10 days old, 30 days overdue, 60 days overdue.

All-suite – A level of service provided by a hotel for a guest who will desire an at-home atmosphere.

Amenities – Personal toiletry items such as shampoo, toothpaste, mouthwash and electrical equipment.

Amenity – A service or item offered to guests or placed in guestrooms for convenience and comfort, at no extra cost.

American plan – A room rate that includes meals, usually breakfast and evening meals as well as room rental in the room rate.

Antique – Antique furniture belongs to the period before 1840, though nowadays any piece of furniture that is more than 100 years old is considered an antique.

Area inventory list – A list of all items and surfaces within a particular area that require the attention of the housekeeping personnel.

Assets – Items that have monetary value

Atrium concept – A design in which guest rooms overlook the lobby from the first floor to the roof.

Authority – The formal power granted by an organization to a management position.

Average Daily Rate (ADR) – A measure of the hotel staff's ability to sell available room rates

Back of the house – The functional areas of the hotel in which employees have little or no guest contact, such as the engineering and maintenance department, laundry room and so on.

Back to back – Describes a heavy rate of check-outs and check-ins on the same day, so that as soon as the room is made up, a new guest checks into it.

Balance sheet – An official financial listing of assets, liabilities and owner's equity.

Bank card – credit cards issued by banks, examples of which include Visa, MasterCard, JCB.

Banquet – A term used to describe catering for specific numbers of people at specific times, in a variety of dining layouts.

Banquet sheet – a listing of the details of an event at which food and beverage are served.

Baseline measurement – A measurement used as a basis for comparisons or for control purposes; a beginning point in an evaluation of output observed over a period of time. A baseline measurement represents how a process performs prior to any improvement effort.

Bath linen – Include bath towels, hand towels, face towels, washcloths and fabric bath mats. Machine.

Behaviour-based interviewing – A technique used by interviewers to determine how applicants have behaved under specific circumstances in the past. The theory behind behaviour-based interviewing is that the best predictor of future behaviour is past behaviour.

Bill-to-account – An extension of credit to a guest by an individual hotel that requires the guest or the guest's employer to establish a line of credit and to adhere to a regular payment schedule

Biometrics – An individual electronic measurement of the uniqueness of a human being such as voice, handprint or facial characteristics.

Blackout – Total loss of electricity.

Blocking on the horizon – Reserving guest rooms in the distant future.

Blocking procedure – Process of reserving a room on a specific day.

Bonsai – Literally meaning "a plant in a tray" this refers to a tree or a plant whose typical growth in nature has been copied exactly in a miniature style within the confines of a container.

Bottom-up – A sales method that involves presenting the least expensive rate first.

Brainstorming – An idea gathering technique that uses team interaction or generates as many ideas as possible within a given time period. Brainstorming taps into the collective brainpower of the team and yields greater results than could be achieved if each individual in the team worked alone.

Breakfast knob cards – Card hung by guests on the knobs of guest room doors to pre-order breakfast at night so that the order reaches the staff on time and the guest is not disturbed for placing the order early in the morning.

Brownouts – Partial loss of electricity.

Budget – A budget is a plan that projects both the revenue that the hotel anticipates during the period covered by the budget and the expenses required to generate the anticipated revenues.

Buff – To smooth the floor with low-speed floor polishing.

Burnishing – Polishing the floor with a high-speed floor machine to achieve an extremely high gloss.

Business affiliation – Chain or independent ownership of hotels.

Cabana – A room adjacent to the pool area, with or without sleeping facilities, but with provision for relaxing on a sofa. It is mainly used for changing.

Call accounting – A computerized system that allows for automatic tracking and posting of outgoing guest room calls.

Cancellation code – A sequential series of alphanumeric combinations that provide the guest with a reference for a cancellation of a guaranteed reservation.

Capital budgets – These allocate the use of capital assets that have a life span considerably in excess of one year, these are assets that are not normally used up in the day to day operations.

Cash bank – A specific amount of paper money and coins issued to a cashier to be used for making change.

Cashier – A person who processes guest check outs and legal tender and make change for guest.

Cashier's report – A daily cash control report that list cashier activity of cash and credit cards and machine totals by cashier shift.

Chain – A group of hotels that follow standard operating procedures such as marketing, reservations, quality of service, food and beverage operations, housekeeping and accounting.

Chain affiliations – Hotels that purchase operational and marketing service from a corporation.

Chain of command – A series of management position in order of authority. An organization's chain of command is represented on an organization chart by lines of authority linking all positions within the organization and specifying formal reporting relationships.

Channel management – Objective review of the most profitable marketing approach for guest rooms, central reservation system, GDS, third party reservation system, toll free phone reservation, travel agent, etc.

City ledger account – A collection of accounts receivable of non-registered guests who use the service of the hotel.

Cleaning supplies – Cleaning agents and small cleaning equipment used in the cleaning of guestrooms and public areas in the hotel.

Coaching – A directive process used by a manager to train and orient an employee to the realities of the workplace and to help the employee remove barriers to optimum work performance.

Code of conduct – Expectations of behavior mutually agreed upon by team members.

Collective bargaining unit – A labor union

Commercial cards – Credit cards issued by cooperation, an example of which is Diners Club.

Commercial hotels – Hotels that provide short-term accommodation for travelling guests.

Commercial rate – Room rates for business people who represent a company but do not necessarily have bargaining power because of their infrequent or sporadic pattern of travel.

Communication hierarchy – A listing of the order in which management personnel may be called on to take charge in an emergency situation.

Complimentary rate – A rate in which there is no charge to the guest.

Computer supplies – Paper, forms, ribbons, ink cartridges needed to operate the system.

Concierge – A person who provides an endless array of information on entertainment, sports, amusement, transportation, tours, church services and babysitting in a particular city or town.

Condominiums – hotels similar to timeshare hotels. The difference between the two lies in the type of ownership. Units in condominium hotels have only one owner instead of multiple owners, each for a limited amount of time each year.

Conference call – A conversation in which three or more persons are linked by telephone.

Confirmed reservations – Prospective guests who have a reservation for accommodations that is honoured until a specified time.

Conflict Management – A process in which a manager attempts to resolve a conflict by applying listening skills, feedback skills and one or more of a variety of conflict-management strategies.

Continental breakfast – Juice , fruit, sweet roll and/or cereal.

Continues improvement – The on going efforts within a company to meet the needs and exceed the expectations of customers by changing the way work is performed so that products and services are delivered better, faster and at least cost than in the past.

Controller – The internal accountant for the hotel.

Convention – A formal assembly of representatives sharing a common field of interest, come together to air their views.

Convention guests – Guest who attend a large convention and receive a special room rate.

Corporate client – A hotel guest who represents a business or is a guest of that business and provides the hotel with an opportunity to establish a regular flow of business during sales periods that would normally be flat.

Corporate guests – frequent guests who are employed by a company and receive a special room rate.

Corporate rates – Room rate offered to corporate clients staying in the hotel.

Coverlet – A bedspread that just covers the top of the dust ruffle but does not reach down to the floor.

Credit – A decrease in an asset or an increase in liability, or an amount of money the hotel owes the guest.

Credit balance – Amounts of money a hotel owes guests in future services.

Credit card imprinter – makes an imprint of the credit card the guest will use as the method of payment.

Crib – Cot for babies, provided to guests on request.

Crisis management – maintaining control of an emergency situation.

Cross-functional team – A team of individuals from different organizational units or functions that solves problems and develops solution effecting the organization as a system.

Cross-training – training employees for performing multiple tasks and jobs.

Current guests – Guest who are registered in the hotel

Customer relationship management – A system that allows hotel managers to integrate technology to support customer service techniques that provide top-notch customer service.

Cycle of service – The progression of a guest's request for products and service through a hotel's department.

Daily blocking – assigning guests to their particular rooms on a daily basis.

Daily sales report – A financial activity report produced by a department in a hotel that reflects daily sales activities with accompanying cash register tapes or point-of-sales audit tapes.

Damp-dust – A method of cleaning where the item to be cleaned is wiped with a damp cloth.

Data sorts – Report option in a PMS that indicate groupings of information.

Database interfaces – the sharing of information among computers.

Debit – An increase in an asset or a decrease in a liability.

Debit balance – An amount of money the guest owes the hotel.

Debit cards – Embossed plastic cards with a magnetic strip on the reverse side that authorize direct transfer of fund from a customer's bank account to the commercial organization's bank account for purchase of goods and services.

Deep cleaning – A thorough cleaning on furniture and accessories, windows, flooring and walls.

Deep cleaning – intensive or specialized cleaning undertaken in guestrooms or public areas, often conducted according to a special schedule or on a special project basis.

Defection rate – A measure of guest dissatisfaction, expresses as a percentage of guest lost to competitors because of service related problems.

Demographic data – Size, density, distribution, and vital statistics of population broken down into, for example; age, sex, marital status and occupation categories.

Departmental accounts – Income and expense-generating areas of the hotel, such as restaurants, gift shops and banquet.

Direct-email letters – Letter sent directly to individuals in a targeted market group in a marketing effort.

Directive communication style – A communication style that combines high dominance with low sociability, characterized by frankness, determination and a no-nonsense approach.

Distance learning – learning that takes place via satellite broadcasts, Picture Tel, or online computer interaction.

DNCO – This room status means that the guest made arrangement s to settle his/her account but has left without informing the front office.

DND Card – A do not disturb card is hung outside the room to inform hotel staff or visitor that the occupant does not wish to be disturb.

Double Locked (DL) – An occupied room in which the deadbolt has been turn to prohibit entry from the corridor. Only a grandmaster key or an emergency key can open it.

Double Occupancy Percentage – A measure of a hotel's staff ability to attract more than one guest to a room

Driving force – A force that tends to encourage change in a particular direction.

Dry Cleaning – The cleaning of fabrics in a substantially non-aqueous liquid medium.

Duplex – A two storey suite with parlour and bedrooms connected by a stairway.

Dutch wife – Another term for the sewing kit provided as a guest amenity.

Duvet – Quilts filled with down feather or synthetic fibres. Many hotels use duvets with a decorative duvet cover in lieu of both blankets and bedspread. They are sometimes referred to as comforters.

Eco-tourists – Tourist who plan vacation to understand the culture and environment of a particular area

Electronic key – A plastic key with electronic codes embedded on a magnetic strip.

Electronic key system – A system composed of battery-powered or, less frequently, hardwired locks; a host computer and terminals; a keypuncher; and special entry cards that are used as keys.

Empowerment – Management's act of delegating certain authority and responsibility to frontline employees.

Empowerment – The redistribution of power within an organization that enables managers, supervisors, and employees to perform their jobs more efficiently and effectively with the overall goal of enhancing service to guests and increasing profits for the organization by releasing decision-making responsibility, authority and accountability to every level within the organization.

EPABX Operator – Electronic Private Automatic Branch Exchange operators. These are the hotel switchboard operators who answer calls and connect them to the appropriate extensions. These operators also relay telephone charges incurred by guests to the front office cashier.

Ergonomics – The study of how people relate psychologically to machines.

European plan – A rate that quotes room charge only.

Exhaust vent – An opening for ventilation, sometimes fixed with an exhaust fan to facilitate of fresh air.

Express check out – Means by which the guest uses computer technology in a guest room or a computer in the hotel lobby to check out.

Family rate – room rates offered to encourage visit by families with children.

FFE – Furniture, Fixtures and Equipment.

Fix assets – These are tangible assets of a long term nature, such as land or large pieces of machinery and equipments.

Fixture – Hardware items present in guestrooms that cannot be moved or are difficult to move as a whole since they are fixed in position. For example; wash basin, baths and lighting fixtures.

Float – The delay in payment from an account after using a credit card or personal check.

Floatels – Hotel establishments being operated on large water bodies such as seas and lakes. Cruise liner and some houseboats are typical examples of these.

Floor limit – A dollar amount set by the credit card agency that allows for a maximum amount of guest charges.

Floor pantry – A service room provided on each floor for GRAs to store cleaning agents, equipments, guest supplies, guest room linen and maid's cart.

Flow analysis processes – The preparation of a schematic drawing of the operations included in a particular function.

Flowchart – An analysis of the delivery of a particular product or service.

Folio – A guest's record of charges and payment.

Force field analysis – A planning technique that helps you identify and visualize the relationships of significant forces that influence a situation, problem or goal.

Forecasting – Projecting room sales for a specific period.

Forming – The first stage of team development, characterized by cautions, limited member participation, dependence on the leader and low productivity.

Front of the house – The functional areas of the hotel in which employees have extensive guest contact, such as food and beverage outlets and front office areas.

Full house – 100 percent hotel occupancy; a hotel that has all its guest room occupied.

Full service – A level of service provided by a hotel with a wide range of conveniences for the guest.

Gate pass – An authorization given to an employee to take guest or hotel property out of the hotel.

General ledger – A collection of accounts that the controller uses to organize the financial activities of the hotel.

Global Distribution System (GDS) – Distributor of hotel rooms to corporations such as travel agents that buy rooms in large volume.

Goal Setting – A process in which objectives are created to improve one's work performance or personal skills.

Going green – the responsibility to take care of the environment.

Graveyard shift – Night shift.

Group rate – Room rate offered to large groups of people visiting the hotel for a common reason.

Group travellers – People who are travelling on business or for pleasure in an organized fashion.

Groupthink – The tendency of a group to stifle differences of opinion in an effort to preserve group unity and harmony; may arise during the norming stage of team development.

Guaranteed reservations – Prospective guests who made a contact with the hotel for a guest room.

Guest essentials – items that are essential to the guestrooms and are not expected to be used up or taken away by guest.

Guest expendables – Guest supplies that are expected to be used up or taken away by guest on leaving the property.

Guest Folio – A form imprinted with the hotel's logo and control number and allowing space for room number, guest identification, date in and date out, and room rate in the upper left-hand corner; it allows for guest charges to be imprinted with PMS and is filed in room number sequence.

Guest histories – Detail concerning the guest' visits, such as ZIP code, frequent of visits, corporate affiliation or special needs.

Guest Loan Items – Guest supplies not normally found in a guestrooms but available upon request. For example; ironing board.

Guest supplies – Commonly referred to as guest amenities or personal toiletries; care items such as small bottles of shampoo, hair conditioner, lotion, soap, mouthwash, shoeshine cloth, mending kit etc.

Guest supplies – These are items placed in the guestroom free of cost for the use and comfort of guest.

Hand caddy – A portable container for storing and transporting cleaning supplies, carried on a room maid's cart.

Handle with care (HWC) guest – Guest who may have had some unpleasant experiences in the hotel or had some complaints, genuine or otherwise, are labeled as " handle with care " guest by the hotel for the reminder of their stay or future sojourn.

Hard key system – A security devise consisting of the traditional hard key that fits into keyhole in a lock; preset tumblers inside the lock are turned by the designated key.

Hard water – Water that contains more than 60 ppm (part per million) of calcium and/or magnesium is called hard water.

Hardware – Computer equipment used to process software, such as central processing units, keyboards, monitor and printers.

Hollywood Twin room – A room with two twin beds but a common headboard, which is meant for two people. If the need arises, the beds can be bridged together to make it appear a single bed.

Hospitality – The cordial and generous reception and entertainment of guests or strangers, either socially or commercially.

Hospitality – The generous and cordial provision of services to a guest.

Hotel representative – A member of the marketing and sales department of the hotel who actively seeks out group activities planner.

House count – The number of persons registered in a hotel on a specific night.

Housekeeping room status – Terminology that indicate s availability of guest room such as available, clean or ready (room is ready to be occupied),

occupied (guest or guests are already occupying a room), dirty or stay over (guest will not be checking out of a room on the current day), on change (guest has checked out of the room, but housekeeping staff has not released the room for occupancy), and out of order (the room is not available for occupancy because of a mechanical malfunction)

Hubbart formula – A method used to computed room rate that considers such factors as operating expenses, desired return on investment and income from various departments in the hotel.

Incentive program – An organized effort by management to understand employees' motivational concerns and develop opportunities for employees to achieve both their goals and the goals of the hotel.

Independent hotel – A hotel that is not associated with a franchise.

In-house laundry – A hotel-operated department that launders linens, uniforms, bedspreads etc.

In-room guest check out – A feature of the property management system that allows the guest to use a guest room television to check out of a hotel.

Interdepartmental communication – Communication between departments.

Interfacing – The ability of computers to communicate electronically and share data.

Inter-hotel property referrals – A system in which one member-property recommends another member property to a guest.

Internal moment of truth – A specific event, situation, or interaction in which anyone employed by a company comes into contact with some aspect of the company that contribute to the quality of his or her work experience.

Inventory – Stock or merchandise, operating supplies, and other items held for future use in a hotel. For example; linen, cleaning supplies and so on, are important housekeeping inventories.

Jacuzzis – Whirlpool ; small pools in which alternate jets of warm water bring about therapeutic effect.

Job analysis – A detailed listing of the tasks performed in a job, which provides the basis for a sound job description.

Job description – A listing of required duties to be performed by an employee in a particular job.

Just in time training – A process that provides training when it is needed.

Key drawer – A drawer located underneath the counter of the front desk that holds room keys in slots in numerical order.

Key fob – A decorative and descriptive plastic or metal tag attached to a hard key.

King-size bed – The largest size of bed available, with dimension of 78 inches x 80 inches (eastern king) or 72 x 80 inches (California king)

Laissez faire – A style of leadership where a leader believes in delegating assignments and important task to others in the team.

Lanai – A room overlooking a landscaped area, a scenic view, a water body or garden. It may have a balcony, a patio or both.

Landscape area – An area where trees, plants, turf, deck, walks, ponds and so on have been used to create a natural looking outdoor space that is functional and visually appealing.

Late charges – Guest charges that might not be included on the guest folio because of a delay in posting by other department.

Lateral communication – Communication with those on the same level as you in the organization.

Leisure travellers – People who travel alone or with others on their own for visits to points of interest, to relatives, or for other personal reasons.

Liabilities – Financial or other contractual obligations or debts.

Limited service – A level of service provided by a hotel with guest room accommodations and limited food service and meeting space.

Linen chute – A passage in the form of a tunnel for sending soiled linen from the floor pantries of all floors to a central place near the laundry, from where it can be collected by the laundry staff.

Litigious society – An environment in which consumers sue providers of products and services for not delivering them according to expected operating standards.

Luggage rack – A furniture item provided in guestrooms for placing the guest's luggage on.

Make up – servicing of the room while a guest is registered in the room.

Manager's report – A listing of occupancy statistics from the previous day, such as occupancy percentage, yield percentage, average daily rate, Rev PAR, and number of guests.

Market segment – Identifiable group of customers with similar needs for products and services.

Marquee – The curbside message board, which includes the logo of the hotel and space for a message.

Mass marketing – Advertising products and service through mass communications such as television, radio, and internet.

Material Safety Data Sheets (MSDS) – A listing of the chemical contents, relative hazards to the users, and name and address of the producers of the contents.

MICE – Meeting, incentives, conventions, exhibitions. This segment is now a big revenue generator for the hotels. Certain hotels cater specially to the MICE customer.

Military and Educational rate – Room rate established for military personnel and educators.

Mini bar – A fixture in modern guestrooms, this is a miniature refrigerator stocked with juices, liquor, and snack for the convenience of guests.

Minutes – A written summary of the events and actions of a meeting.

Mission statement – A statement of the mission of an organization or team that describes the organizations or team's reason for existence. Mission statements are broad and expected to remain in effect for an extended period of time.

Modified American Plan – A room rate that offers one meal with the price of a room rental.

Moment of truth – Any episode in which a customer comes into contact with some aspect of an organization and gets an impression of the quality of its service: considered to be the basic atom of service, the smallest indivisible unit of value delivered to customer.

Moonlighter – A person who holds a full-time job at one organization and a part-time job at another organization.

Motels – Hotels that are located primarily on highways. They provide modest lodgings to highways travelers. Most motels provide ample parking space and may be located near a petrol station.

Murphy bed – This refers to a bed that folds up into the walls and looks like a bookshelf or cupboard when folded away, being named for a leading manufacturer of such beds. It may also be called a Sico bed (after another leading manufacturer of foldaway or wall beds)

Networking – The practice of developing personal connections with friends, acquaintance, colleagues, associates, teacher, counselor and others.

Night Audit – the control process whereby the financial activity of guest's accounts is maintained and balanced on a daily basis.

Nightstand – A nightstand is a small stand or cabinet designed to stand beside a bed or elsewhere in a bedroom, as a place to put anything likely to be required during the night; also called night table.

Norming – The third stage of team development, during which relationships become cooperative and supportive as members learn that they can work together as a cohesive unit. The team becomes more productive during this stage.

No-show factor – Percentage of guests with confirmed or guaranteed reservations who do not show up.

Occupancy percentage – The number of rooms sold devided by the number of rooms available.

On change room – A room in need of housekeeping service before it can be registered to an arriving guest.

On the job training – A training process in which the employee observes and practices a tasks while performing his or her job.

OOO – Out of Order is the status of a guestroom that is not rentable because it is being repaired or redecorated.

Open section – A group of rooms that is not part of a room section for cleaning purposes.

Operating Budgets – These forecast the expense and revenues for the routine operations of the hotel during a certain period.

Operating expenses – Those costs that the hotel incurs in order to generate revenue in the normal course of doing business.

Operating supplies – The items essential to day-to-day housekeeping operations, including guest supplies and cleaning supplies.

OPL – On premises laundry. An in house area in the hotel where linen and uniforms are washed, dry-cleaned and pressed.

Organization Chart – Schematic drawing that list management position in an organization.

Orientation Check List – A summary of all items that must be covered during orientation.

Outsourcing – Provision of service to the hotel, for example; a central reservation system by an agency outside of the hotel.

Outstanding balance report – A listing of guest's folio balances.

Overbooking – Accepting reservations for more rooms than are available by forecasting the number of no show reservations, stayovers, understays, and walk ins, with the goal of attaining 100 percent occupancy.

Package Rate – Room rate that include goods and services in addition to rental of a room.

Paid in advance (PIA) – Guest who paid cash at check in.

Paid-outs – Amount of monies paid out of the cashier's drawer on behalf of guest or an employee of the hotel.

Par level – The standard number of each inventoried item that must be in hand to support daily, routine housekeeping operations.

Par System – A level of inventory established that provides adequately for service.

Pat stock / par number – A multiple of the standard quantity of a particular inventory item that must be on hand to support daily, routine housekeeping operations.

Percent Yield – The number of rooms sold at average daily rate versus number of rooms available at rack rate multiplied by 100

Performance standards – The quality level that employees' performance is required to meet.

Performing – The fourth stage of team development, during which a team achieves its peak productivity: individual members share the desire to achieve the team's common goals and appreciate each other's individual contributions toward that end.

Pick up rooms – Rooms from the open section assigned to different GRAs to balance out the workload.

Point of sale – An outlet in the hotel that generates income such as a restaurant, gift shop, spa etc.

Policy and procedure manual – Publication that provides an outline of how the specific duties of each job are to be performed.

Porch – A covered approach to the entrance of a building.

Posting – The process of debiting and crediting charges and payments to a guest folio.

Potential gross income – The amount of sales a hotel might obtain at a given level of occupancy, average daily rate and anticipated yield.

Power – The ability to influence the behavior of others.

Pre-Opening Budgets – These budget allocate resources for opening parties, advertising, initial generation of goodwill, liaisons and PR. Pre-opening budgets also include the initial costs of employees' salaries and wages, supplies, crockery, cutlery and other such items.

Principle negotiation – A process that helps conflicting parties resolve conflicts in such a way that all parties gain something from the resolution. Four keys to principled negotiation are to separate the people from the problem, focus on what people really mean, invent options for mutual gain, and use objective criteria.

Private label cards – Credit cards issued by retail organization, such as a department store or gasoline company.

Process consultation – A process for resolving conflict that emphasizes understanding the attitudes the conflicting parties hold toward one another. Process consultation attempts to improve the relationship between the parties to the point that they can resolve the conflict themselves.

Productivity standards – The quantity of work expected to be completed by each department employee.

Profit-and-loss statement – A listing of revenues and expenses for a certain time period.

Property Management System (PMS) – A generic term for applications of computer hardware and software used to manage a hotel by networking reservation and registration databases, point of sales system, accounting system and other office software.

Quality service – Service that consistently meet or exceeds customer expectation.

Queen size bed – A queen size bed has the dimensions 5 ft 6 in x 6 ft 6 in.

Rack rate – The highest room rate category offered by a hotel.

Reengineering – An organization change that involves the complete redesign of a process within the organization, the goal of which is to achieve a dramatic improvement.

Referral reservation service – A service offered by a management company of a chain of hotels to franchisee members.

Refurbish – To give a new look to a room by re-decorating, renewing soft furnishings, and possibly changing the carpet and touching up the furniture.

Registration card – A form on which the guest indicates name, home or billing address, phone number, date of departure, method of payment and etc.

Reinvention – An extreme organizational change requiring an organization to rethink every aspect of how it conducts business.

Residential hotel – hotels that provide long term accommodations for guest.

Restraining force – A force that tends to keep a situation from changing in a particular direction.

Revenue management – A process of planning to achieve maximum room rate and most profitable guests (guest who will spend money at the hotel's food and beverage outlets, spa etc) that encourages front office manager, general manager and marketing or sales director to target sales periods and develop sales programs that will maximize profit for the hotel.

Room assignment sheets – The room assignment sheet indicates the rooms that the particular GRA has to service, giving their status as indicates in the daily work report. The sheet also lists any pick up rooms that the GRA has to service, apart from the rooms in his/her section.

Room blocking – reserving rooms for guests who are holding reservations.

Room revenue – The amount of room sales received.

Room sales projections – A weekly report prepared and distributed by the front office manager that indicates the number of the departures, arrivals, walk ins, stayovers, and no shows.

Room section – A group of 15-16 guestrooms reasonably contiguous to each other.

Room status discrepancy – A situation in which the housekeeping department's description of a room's status differs from the room status information with the front office.

Room status report – A report that allows the housekeeping department to identify the occupancy or condition of the property's rooms. It is generated daily through a two-way communication between housekeeping and front office.

Runners – In this context, lengths of matting made of synthetic or natural fibers, placed at entrances to prevent dirt and dust from entering the building. (Another use of the term runner in housekeeping is for a person who is charged with the duty of conveying orders from housekeeping department to the staff on guest floor).

Safety stock level – The number of purchase unit that must always be on hand in case of emergencies, damages, delays in delivery and so on.

Sales indicators – Number of guest and revenue generated.

Sani-bin – These are small metal or plastic containers with lids, kept in toilets for collection of soiled sanitary towels.

Scanty baggage – A room status indicating a room assigned to guest with small, light and few pieces of luggage that could be carried away without obviously indicating a departure, should a guest walk out with them.

Self-check-in process – A procedure that requires the guest to insert a credit card with a magnetic stripe containing personal and financial data into a self check in terminal and answer a few simple questions concerning the guest stay.

Self-directed team – A work team that manages itself and its work, making job assignments, planning work schedules and making service and production related decision.

Service directory – This is a booklet in which the services offered to guests by the hotel are listed, along with the intercom numbers to reach the relevant departments.

Service recovery system – Policies and procedures that guide manager and staff in resolving guest complaint.

Service strategy – The effort of a hospitality business to increase guest perceptions of value by consistently meeting or exceeding important guest expectations in critical moment of truth.

Skipper – A room status that indicates the guest has left the hotel without making arrangements to settle his/her account.

Sleeper – A room status means that the guest has settle his/her account and left the hotel but the front office staff have failed to update the room status.

Soft water – Water in which the level of dissolved calcium and/or magnesium is below 60 ppm.

Soiled linen – Dirty and stained linen that required laundering.

Sorting – The process of separating soiled linen into different categories: those requiring dry-cleaning and those that should be laundered under different conditions, such as whites and colored. In other words, sorting is governed construction and the amount and kind of soil.

Spotting – The specialized function of stain removal carried out by skilled personal called spotters, using appropriate equipment and stain-removal agents.

Stain – A spot or discoloration left on fabrics from contact with and absorption of foreign substances.

Stayovers – currently registered guest who wish to extend their stay beyond the time for which they made reservations.

Stock taking – The physical verification of inventory items by counting up stocks of all items at periodic intervals. Stock taking is also termed "conducting inventory ".

Storming – The second stage of team development, characterized by conflict within the group as team members push boundaries and challenge authority. Member interaction becomes confrontational and productivity remains low.

Studio bed – this is dual purpose bed that is used as divan in the daytime and converts into a bed in the night after the removal of bolsters and covers.

Supportive communication style – A communication style that combines high sociability with low dominance, characterized by sensitivity, patience and preference for informal interactions.

Surveillance equipment – Equipment such as CCTVs (Closet circuit televisions) that help to closely observe suspicious activities and persons.

Swab cloth – A soft, absorbent cleaning cloth used for wet cleaning work, such as for wash basin, baths, and so on.

SWB – Salaries, Wages and Benefit.

SWOT analysis – A brainstorming technique. "SWOT" stands for Strengths, Weakness, Opportunity and Threats.

Task-force team – A temporary work team formed to solve a specific problem that usually involves several departments or areas within an organization.

Tent cards – Hotel publicity cards in the shape of tents placed in guestrooms.

Terrazzo – Flooring which consists of marble, granite and other decorative chips set in cement.

Timeshares – vacation interval hotels. These involve individuals purchasing the ownership of accommodations for a specific period of time, usually one or two weeks a year. These owner then can occupy the unit during that time. Owner may also have the unit rented out by the management company that operates the hotel.

Tooth glass – A glass placed on the vanity unit as a guest supply and used for gargling or to keep the guest's toothbrush, dentures, or other similar items in.

Total Quality Management (TQM) – A management technique that encourages managers to look critically at process used to produce products and services.

Transforming – The fifth and final stage of team development, when the group is either preparing to disband or facing a major change in its mission, membership, or environment. The team often regresses to behaviors characteristic of earlier stage of development as it struggles to cope with the changes.

Travel directories – Organized listings of hotel reservation access methods and hotel geographic and specific accommodations information.

Traveller's checks – Prepaid checks that have been issued by a bank or other financial organization.

Turn down service – A special service provided by the housekeeping department in which a room attendant enters the guestroom early in the evening to re stock supplies, tidy the room and turn down the covers on the bed in preparation for the night.

Understays – Guest who arrive on time but decide to leave before their predicted date of departure.

Upsell – To encourage a customer to consider buying a higher priced product or service than originally anticipated.

Upward communication – Communication with those above you in the organization.

Vacant – The status of a room in which no guest has slept the previous night and which is not yet occupied.

Vanity area – A unit comprising a wash basin and mirror, surrounded by flat area where soap, dental kits, shaving kits, and tooth glasses are kept.

Vision statement – A company's assertion of the direction, objectives and ethical code underlying its purpose for being.

Visual alarm systems – flashing lights that indicate a fire or other emergency in a hotel room.

Walk-in guest – Guest who request a room rental without having made a reservation.

Water closet – Sanitary fitting consisting of the toilet bowl and the cistern.

Wi-fi – Wireless fidelity. This is an amenity provided nowadays by world-class hotels. Wi-fi enables guests to access a wide range of information, applications, and computing resources without connectivity problems.

Yield – The percentage of income that could be secured if 100 percent of available rooms are sold at their full rack rate.

Zero base budgeting – Zero base budgeting refers to hiring employees while taking into account the actual occupancy for a specified period of time.